ACROSS THE PARK
EVERTON FC & LIVERPOOL FC
COMMON GROUND

BY PETER LUPSON

ACKNOWLEDGEMENTS

I am indebted to a number of people who have given me invaluable assistance in writing this book. Without their help, the materials I have been able to draw upon would have been sadly depleted and the task of trying to produce something worthwhile would have been a massive, uphill struggle.

One absolutely indispensable resource was the David France Collection in the Liverpool Record Office. The range and depth of this collection is literally breathtaking. The extensive archives, artefacts and medals offer profound insights not only into the history of Everton and Liverpool but also football in general. I would like to thank Max Dunbar for making the collection available to me, in particular the joint Everton-Liverpool match programmes and the priceless ledgers. My requests for particular items were always met with promptness, efficiency and cheerfulness. I would also like to thank Paul Wharton of the Everton Shareholders' Association for helping me to sift through the materials and for uncovering very valuable information. Paul has also given me helpful and encouraging feedback on my writing.

Thanks, too, to George Orr, another member of the Everton Shareholders' Association, for permission to use his quote about John Moores in the fanzine *Blue Blood* of which he is editor. I am grateful to George for his support and encouragement.

Liverpool FC's historian and statistician, Eric Doig, kindly sent me details of players' records that were invaluable for my research for chapter 14. I would also like to thank Eric for reading samples of my work and for his helpful and encouraging feedback. Thanks, too, to another Liverpool FC statistician, Jonny Stokkeland of Norway, for permission to use his photograph of the grave of John McKenna.

I have received an enormous amount of help from Les Rawlinson, archivist and librarian of the *Daily Post* and *Liverpool Echo*. Les often located articles, documents and pictures for me at a moment's notice. Nothing was too much trouble for him. He also kept my spirits up with regular supplies of coffee when my mind went numb from reading too many microfilms. Very much appreciated, Les.

Chris Ledwidge, proprietor of Monuscript Stonemasons of Mirfield, West Yorkshire, did a magnificent job restoring the grave of the Reverend Ben Swift Chambers. Chris kept a detailed photographic record of the restoration process and made these excellent photos available to me. Thank you, Chris.

I am very grateful to Kathleen Parry for the interest she has taken in this book and for obtaining family photographs for me featuring St Domingo Chapel. Kathleen has been a constant source of encouragement throughout. My grateful thanks also to her sisters, Edna Skillicorn and Maureen Ewan, for taking the trouble to send me photographs relating to my research. They were greatly appreciated.

Gwynneth Rowe very kindly allowed me to have photographs of her parents from the time when her late father was minister of St Domingo Chapel. I also want to thank Gwynneth and her sister, Betty Yorke, for sharing their fascinating reminiscences of St Domingo's in the 1930s with me.

Feedback is a vital part of the writing process and I want to thank a number of people, in addition to those already mentioned, who have given me an honest assessment of my work as it has been fed through to them. My wife, Evelyn, always responded cheerfully whenever a sheaf of paper was thrust into her hands to read, usually at times when she had other things to do. Thanks for your encouragement and tolerance, especially when my elastic day shift once again extended into the night. Many thanks, too, to my daughter Karen, my son Mike, Paul Kelly, Rick Parry, Ernie Phillips and Jon Richardson for taking the trouble to read sample chapters of the book and for their helpful and encouraging comments. Ernie Phillips also kindly allowed me to use his photograph of the Everton and Liverpool players at Ben Chambers' graveside in Shepley. Special thanks to Bishop Tom Williams for permission to use the photograph of St Domingo House and for his very warm response to the chapters he read.

It is only too easy to leave people out who deserve a mention. If I am guilty of this, please accept my sincere apologies. If you let me know, I will rectify this in any future printing.

DEDICATION

For my grandson, Daniel Robertson.

May you and your generation carry on the spirit of
goodwill that this book is all about.

*"When you look at the history of both clubs and how they started, Ben Swift Chambers was so
influential. This is an ideal opportunity for us to get together and remember that. The
relationship between the fans has deteriorated to an extent, but if we can show them there's a
unity going back all those years, maybe we can restore some of that."*

Graeme Sharp

*"It has reminded me of the wonderful rapport between Everton and Liverpool fans over so
many years."*

Brian Hall

Produced by Sport Media, Trinity Mirror North West

Across The Park
Design: Jamie Dunmore
Production: Michael Haydock

Executive Editor: Ken Rogers
Editor: Steve Hanrahan
Production Editor: Paul Dove
Art Editor: Rick Cooke
Sub-editors: James Cleary, Roy Gilfoyle, Michael Haydock, Adam Oldfield
Designers: Lee Ashun, Lisa Critchley, Jamie Dunmore, Alison Gilliland, Glen Hind, James Kenyon,
Barry Parker, Colin Sumpter
Writers: Simon Hughes, William Hughes, John Hynes, Alan Jewell, Gavin Kirk,
Chris McLoughlin, David Randles
Sales and Marketing Manager: Elizabeth Morgan

Published in Great Britain in 2008 by: Trinity Mirror Sport Media,
PO Box 48, Old Hall Street, Liverpool L69 3EB

ISBN: 9781906802127

Photographs: Peter Lupson, Trinity Mirror, PA Photos

Printed by PCP

CONTENTS

INTRODUCTION
ACROSS THE PARK

Passion! No word better characterises the intense depth of feeling that the football public associates with the supporters of Merseyside's two illustrious football clubs, Everton and Liverpool. Across the years, the proud wearers of both blue and red have been energised by the fervour of their supporters. It has provided them with the fuel that has propelled them to heights of glory that most other clubs can only dream of. Whether at the pinnacle of English league football, in FA Cup or League Cup finals, or on the European stage, Everton and Liverpool have made their presence felt.

Some have suggested that the passion of their supporters has sectarian roots, Everton allegedly being the Catholic club and Liverpool the Protestant one. But this is quite wrong, as will be explained later in the book. In fact, far from being divided by sectarian or any other kind of social or political loyalties, the two clubs share a common heritage and have enjoyed a degree of harmony and understanding unmatched between clubs in other major UK cities.

This book will be a celebration of the good things the two clubs have in common. It will explore their many positive links, starting from their shared roots at St Domingo Chapel in the last quarter of the 19th century to their joint restoration in 2008 of the grave of Ben Chambers, the Methodist minister who set the ball rolling that led to their birth. Of course, the acrimonious split of 1892 and the events leading up to it must not be overlooked but, equally, the amazing gestures of reconciliation that followed it should also be highlighted. Isn't it remarkable, for instance, that at the funeral of John Houlding, the initiator of the split, three Everton and three Liverpool players carried his coffin, and the flags at Anfield and Goodison Park were flown at half-mast?

Neighbours: Goodison and
Anfield face each other
across Stanley Park

Friendly rivalry: Supporters
seated together for the
Merseyside derby in 1998

Isn't it equally remarkable that only two years after Houlding's death the clubs collaborated on the publication of a shared match programme, a joint venture that was to result in over 1,100 issues during the next 31 years? How well known is it that the players and directors of both clubs met together for an annual service called Football Sunday at St Domingo Chapel until the outbreak of the Second World War? Or that 33 players across the years have worn both the blue of Everton and the red of Liverpool? Or even that ownership of both clubs was at one time largely in the hands of a single family?

There is nothing that shows the character of a city more than its response to heart-breaking human tragedies, and Liverpool has certainly had more than its fair share of these. The essential goodwill that exists between the supporters of its two famous clubs was much in evidence in the wake of the Hillsborough disaster of 1989 which claimed the lives of 96 Liverpool supporters. No one can possibly forget the spontaneous outpouring of shared grief in the city, with Everton supporters rallying round their Liverpool counterparts by laying wreaths at Anfield and forming a long continuous line of scarves in the colours of both clubs that stretched from Goodison Park to Anfield. When Everton and Liverpool met in the FA Cup final that season, partisan loyalties were submerged in the chant of "Merseyside! Merseyside! Merseyside!" that rang around Wembley Stadium.

The sense of community expressed by both sets of supporters that day is an indication of the fundamental goodwill that exists between the majority of them. And it is the purpose of this book to capture that spirit and celebrate the marvellous heritage of two great clubs whose history has, to a considerable degree, overlapped.

CHAPTER 1
BEN SWIFT CHAMBERS:
FIRST OF THE SUMMER WINE

The story begins in the village of Shepley, the boyhood home of Ben Swift Chambers who set the ball rolling that led to the birth of Everton and Liverpool Football Clubs. Shepley is in the beautiful rolling West Yorkshire countryside just four miles from Holmfirth where the long-running TV comedy series 'Last of the Summer Wine' was filmed. Unforgettable characters from the series such as Compo, Cleggy and Foggy, together with the inimitable Nora Batty, have become household names and made the area hugely popular with tourists. In contrast, Ben Swift Chambers, a son of this area, has remained a barely known, obscure figure despite his massive contribution to the world of football. Not only has no biography of him ever been written nor any photograph of him been found, but his name wasn't even known to Shepley residents until the re-dedication of his restored grave in the village on Wednesday 2 July 2008 which was attended by players and senior officials of Everton and Liverpool. A full account of his life and of the invaluable contribution he has made to the history of the two great Merseyside clubs is long overdue. It is time to give him the recognition he deserves.

EARLY LIFE IN SHEPLEY
Ben Swift Chambers was born on 30 August 1845 in a weaver's cottage in Stocksmoor, a hamlet a mile from Shepley and about six miles from Huddersfield. At the time of Ben's birth his father, Joah, worked in the cottage as a clothier where he wove cloth for sale to local woollen merchants and textile mills. However, by 1848 and before Ben was three, the family had moved to nearby Shepley, which at the time was a small village with a population of about 1,100. Here Joah became the master and his wife, Maria, the mistress of a school opened in 1834 by the British and Foreign Schools Society to provide non-denominational Christian education for children between the ages of six and 11. Joah, Maria and their family lived in the schoolhouse next to the school during the whole of Ben's childhood and youth. His two brothers and eight sisters were all born there.

CALL TO THE METHODIST MINISTRY
When a chapel belonging to the New Connexion branch of Methodism was opened in Shepley in 1837, no one could possibly have foreseen what a huge part this would play in Ben's life and, ultimately, in the history of Everton and Liverpool Football Clubs. It was here that Ben discovered his calling to the Methodist ministry which would eventually take him to Liverpool. From an early age he taught with such dedication and enthusiasm in the chapel's Sunday School (which still stands in Marsh Lane) that it was predicted by many he would become a clergyman.

Despite his talent for religious teaching, Ben's career started on a completely different track. He began working life as an apprentice to a high-class engraver in Huddersfield where he proved to be so good at his work that his employer offered him a partnership in the business. But the

Nora Batty's house in 'Last of the Summer Wine':
The show was filmed in and around Holmfirth, not far from where Ben Swift Chambers was born

Left: Shepley village today

pull of the Methodist ministry proved too strong and Ben turned down this tempting offer with all its promise of financial security. And so, in 1867 at the age of 22, he duly enrolled as a student at the Methodist College where he began a two-year period of training.

On qualification two years later, he took up his first appointment as a minister in the Ashton-under-Lyne circuit. Methodist ministers were very mobile at the time, spending only short periods in each circuit, so after only one year in Ashton, Ben moved to Stockport for a year before arriving in Halifax in 1871. It was during his two-year period in Halifax that he married Elizabeth Holden, a farmer's daughter from his home village of Shepley. The Holdens were a large, well-established Shepley family, and many of them held positions of responsibility in the New Connexion chapel. Undoubtedly, Ben and Elizabeth would have got to know each other well through their families' respective involvement in the chapel. Their marriage took place on 9 June 1873 in Halifax. Ben was 27, Elizabeth 28.

That same year they moved to Barrow and after two years there, then a further two in Gateshead, they arrived in Liverpool on 1 July 1877 where Ben, now 32, was appointed circuit superintendent and minister of St Domingo Chapel in the Everton district. The histories of Everton and Liverpool were about to begin...

ST DOMINGO CHAPEL, EVERTON

St Domingo's was built in a predominantly middle-class area to replace three existing Methodist New Connexion chapels – Bethesda, Bevington Hill and Chatham Place – whose numbers had drastically fallen. The members of these chapels agreed it would make sense to merge and worship in a single building in a location convenient for them all. A site was chosen at the junction of Breckfield Road North and St Domingo Vale, and building began on 12 September 1870. The foundation stone was laid that day by 55-year-old Joseph Wade, one of its newly appointed trustees and formerly a trustee of Bevington Hill Chapel. Less than a year later, on Sunday 20 July 1871, the first services took place.

Before continuing the story, it is important to correct the widely held but completely mistaken belief that Everton is a Catholic club. One of the reasons for this assumption is the Latin-sounding name of St Domingo Chapel where, as we shall shortly see, the club was born. In fact, the chapel was merely named after the two streets between which it stood, St Domingo Grove and St Domingo Vale. These, in turn, derived their name from an impressive villa on the crest of Everton Hill called St Domingo House which had been built in 1757 by a wealthy Liverpool merchant, George Campbell, from the spoils of a French ship he had captured off the island of Santo Domingo (now the Dominican Republic). He named his villa and its 53-acre estate after the island to commemorate his great prize. In time, the name was adopted by local streets, recreation grounds and

Learning his trade: The Sunday School building in Shepley where Ben Chambers taught as a youth

Left: On the crest of Everton Hill stood St Domingo House, which gave its name to the surrounding area
Right: St Domingo Chapel, which was built to replace three New Connexion chapels in Liverpool

eventually a political ward. Interestingly, St Domingo House was eventually bought by the Unitarians for use as a boys' school, one of whose most famous pupils was the great Liverpool philanthropist, William Rathbone. Later, the building became the home of St Edward's College.

CHAMBERS ARRIVES AT ST DOMINGO'S

The minutes of the chapel's Leaders' Meeting of 20 June 1877 record the preparations for Ben Chambers' arrival. They inform us that his first services on Sunday 1 July and the special tea in the schoolroom the next day to formally welcome him as the new minister were to be advertised on specially designed posters. We also learn that admission to the formal tea was to be restricted to 200 guests at a cost of one shilling (5p) per person, although the poorer members of the chapel would receive free tickets. The choir would be in attendance to mark the importance of the occasion and the young men of the chapel would be asked to wait on at the tables. These young men could not have been aware of the significance of Chambers' arrival: some of them would soon become members of the chapel football club that was to be the cradle of Everton.

From the start, work with young people was considered a vital part of St Domingo's mission, and significantly the Sunday School was built and fully operational before the chapel itself was completed. Chambers, too, was particularly concerned for the welfare of young people and worked hard to further their spiritual and educational development. It didn't take him

long to win the trust of the young members of the chapel, nor indeed that of the older ones. His magnetic personality and good nature quickly drew people to him, and they remained powerful assets throughout his ministry. In the words of the *Methodist New Connexion Conference Minutes* of 1902, he possessed 'a powerful and winning personality' and was a 'manly, affectionate, kindly, pleasant, happy, noble being, eager to serve, anxious to do good, a never-failing friend'.

One of the groups with which he became deeply involved at St Domingo's was the Band of Hope. This group was part of the Band of Hope Union, a national body that had been formed in 1851 to help young people resist the temptation of drink. It organised wholesome recreational activities for young people and taught them about the dangers of drink. Late Victorian England had a massive alcohol problem, and drink-related crime and violence were commonplace. Drink was also responsible for many pitiful cases of child neglect, with money that should have been spent on food and clothing being squandered in the public house. Temperance workers such as Chambers did all they could to oppose the drink culture and prevent the widespread misery it caused.

THE BIRTH OF ST DOMINGO FOOTBALL CLUB

Chambers also had a special affinity with the members of the Young Men's Bible Class in the Sunday School, most of whom were in their late teens. Within only a month of his arrival he had persuaded them to form

Touch of class: These houses (left) show the social level of the St Domingo Chapel area when Chambers was minister there
Above: The row of weavers' cottages in Stocksmoor where Ben Chambers was born

a chapel cricket club. He would have had several reasons for wanting to do this. Apart from the obvious pleasure the sport would give them, he no doubt felt it would also provide them with healthy exercise and the opportunity to deepen their friendship bonds.

But, more importantly, Chambers was an enthusiastic supporter of the 'muscular Christian' movement that spread throughout England in the last quarter of the 19th century. Muscular Christians firmly believed in rolling up their sleeves and getting stuck in to help others. They brought about great improvements in the living conditions of the poor, particularly in the fight against poverty, squalor and poor sanitation. They also placed great value on wholesome outdoor recreational activities as a means of promoting good health and developing strength and physique. Team sports such as cricket and football were believed to be the most effective vehicles for achieving this, but they were seen to have other benefits, too, which were possibly even more important for a young person's welfare. These benefits concerned the development of Christian character, in particular qualities such as courage, fair play, unselfishness and self-control.

In view of his muscular Christian beliefs, Chambers would have been delighted at the enthusiastic response of the Bible Class youths to his proposal to start a cricket club. In no time at all, The St Domingo Cricket Club had been formed and a plot of land had been found in Oakfield Road for use as a pitch. They played their first games there in the summer of

1877. By the following summer they had really caught the bug and decided it would be a good idea to stay fit during the winter months in preparation for the next season. But what could they do to keep in shape during the winter?

It was almost certainly Chambers who suggested they should take up Association football. The game had only been created 15 years previously in 1863 and was still very much in its infancy. It enjoyed no status and couldn't even remotely be considered a rival to cricket, the country's premier sport. In fact, fewer than 100 clubs across the country were members of The Football Association. However, Chambers had probably heard from other sports-minded clergymen in the area that it was a useful form of winter exercise for cricketers.

Very conveniently, Stanley Park with its extensive 93 acres had opened on 14 May 1870, about a year before the first services at St Domingo Chapel were held. It was only a short walk from the chapel and provided ideal playing fields for football. Probably acting on Chambers' recommendation, the Bible Class scholars decided to try out this novel form of recreation and become footballers in the winter of 1878. They chose the south-east corner of the park for their pitch as it was closest to where most of them lived. And to clearly demarcate their sporting activities they decided to re-name themselves St Domingo Football Club in the winter months. Ben Chambers could never have guessed what he had started...

15

CHAPTER 2
FROM ST DOMINGO TO EVERTON

At first the St Domingo youths just played games among themselves. Their football was of a very rudimentary kind, everyone chasing the ball in a mad scramble. It took a while before they felt confident enough to test themselves against other teams. Their earliest recorded match was a 1-0 victory against the Everton United Church Club. It was an unusual club in that it drew its players from four different Anglican churches in the Everton district and included three Anglican clergymen in its squad.

The match was reported in the *Liverpool Daily Courier* on 20 October 1879 in only the briefest terms:

> *'ST DOMINGO v EVERTON CHURCH CLUB (Association). This match was played on the ground of the former, at Stanley-park, on Saturday last, and after a closely contested game victory rested with the St Domingo by one goal to nil.'*

It is noticeable that the word 'Association' appears in brackets after the teams' names. This was to indicate that the match was played according to the rules of Association football and not Rugby football, a much more popular and respected game. The brevity of the report was typical of the period. Association football was not taken seriously as a sport and team line-ups and goalscorers were considered to be of little interest. The few football reports that did appear in the press were usually sent in by club secretaries as there was no coverage by professional reporters as today. Reports of cricket matches, on the other hand, frequently contained full details of players, runs scored and wickets lost.

However, we do know from the first history of the club published in 1893 and written by 'Floreat Evertonae' that matches were also played against St John's (Bootle), St Mary's and St Peter's in the club's first season. Thomas Keates, an early Everton director, adds St Benedict's to the list in his *Jubilee History* of 1878. It will quickly be noticed that St Domingo's opponents were from other churches. This was because churches were the main providers of recreation for young people at the time, in much the same way that youth clubs are today. In fact, by 1885 some 25 of the 112 clubs playing football in Liverpool had links with religious organisations.

The first colours worn by the team were blue and white striped jerseys, but the St Domingo players did not enjoy the luxury of a dressing room to protect them from the elements on matchdays. Nor did they enjoy the services of a groundsman to prepare their pitch. Goalposts were housed in a lodge in the centre of Stanley Park, and if they wanted to use them they had to carry them themselves.

Despite the primitive nature of St Domingo's early play, they were eager learners and, according to Keates, they soon became the best team in Stanley Park. Success breeds success, and before long the better players in

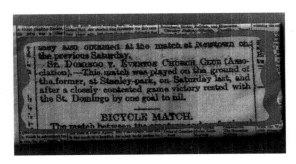

Where it began: St Domingo first played on a segment of Stanley Park next to where Anfield now stands – it is covered by the car park (left). Above: The first St Domingo match report in the *Liverpool Courier*

Redeveloped: The site of St Domingo Chapel today

other clubs were keen to join them. As the season progressed, six were added to their ranks from the Everton United Church Club while four joined from St Peter's. In fact, the situation soon began to cause embarrassment because there were more players in the team from outside St Domingo Chapel than within it.

CHANGE OF NAME TO EVERTON

It seemed that the only solution was a change of name. A committee meeting was held at their headquarters, the Queen's Head Hotel in Village Street, Everton, to discuss the situation. It was unanimously agreed to re-name the club 'The Everton Football Club' after the district in which most of them lived. John Clarke, landlord of the Queen's Head, was appointed secretary.

Despite the removal of the name St Domingo from its title, the club did not sever its links with the chapel. In fact, some of the most prominent and influential figures in Everton's history were also key members of the chapel.

Remarkably, some form of link between chapel and club existed from 1878 until 1948.

Having agreed to a change of name, the committee decided to leave club colours as they were. Although the St Domingo players turned out in blue and white stripes, their recruits from outside continued to play in the colours of their former clubs. This odd mixture on the field of play must have presented a strange sight to spectators and one with which they would have been familiar until October 1881.

The new name was given the best possible baptism with the 6-0 annihilation of St Peter's on 23 December 1879. As with the report of the match between St Domingo and the Everton Church Club two months earlier, there was no mention of team line-ups or goalscorers in the local press. However, in the return match against St Peter's on 24 January 1880 in Stanley Park, when Everton gained a resounding 4-0 victory, the first-known Everton line-up was printed. The team, which played in the customary 2-2-6 formation of the time, was: W Jones (goal); Tom Evans and J Douglas (backs); Charles Hiles and Sidney Chalk (capt) (half-backs); Robert Morris, A White, Frank Brettle, Alfred Wade, Smith and W Williams (forwards).

ALFRED RILEY WADE

Alfred Riley Wade, one of the forwards, was to become an influential Everton director during one of the greatest periods in the club's history. He was the son of St Domingo trustee Joseph Wade, who had been given the honour of laying the foundation stone of the chapel on 12 September 1870. Joseph was born in Halifax in 1815. After marrying Grace Riley there, he left Yorkshire for Liverpool where he established a successful coach-building business. By 1871 he was employing 20 men and seven boys. However, it is for his dedication and loyal service to St Domingo's for which he will be remembered. His commitment to the chapel stretched right back to its very beginning. He helped choose the site for its construction, took part in negotiations for buying the land, oversaw all the building arrangements and gave a large sum of money towards the building costs. He also secured the purchase of 128 Queen's Road for the minister's home.

The youngest of his eight children, Alfred Riley Wade, was born on 5 December 1857 and he, too, became a successful coach-builder. Sadly, Joseph did not live long enough to see Alfred play for Everton as he died in September 1875 at the age of 60 before the club was founded. One of Alfred's most treasured possessions was the silver trowel Joseph had used to lay the foundation stone of St Domingo's. His pride in his father's achievements is clear from the following minutes of the Everton management committee of 17 December 1935 (Alfred was a director at this time).

'Mr AR Wade reminded the Board that the Everton Club originated at St Domingo Church, Everton, in 1878; that his father, the late Joseph Wade, had laid the foundation stone of that Church; & that on that occasion he was presented with a Trowel & Mallet. Mr Wade expressed a wish that the Board, on behalf of the Shareholders, would accept from him these mementoes of that interesting event.

'The Chairman [Will Cuff] on behalf of the Directors & Shareholders, thanked Mr Wade for the offer of this most interesting Souvenir & accepted the gift as a token of the very lengthy connection of himself & his family with the Everton Football Club.'

Foundations: A R Wade (above) and the mallet and trowel used by Joseph Wade when the foundation stone of St Domingo Chapel was laid

Alfred Wade had a long and happy involvement with Everton. Playing for the club in its original form as St Domingo FC, he went on to represent it when it changed its name to Everton FC and he eventually became a director in 1904. He stepped down from this position for an interval but rejoined the board in 1921, remaining on it until his death in 1936 at the age of 78. The League Championship successes of the 1927/28 and 1931/32 seasons, and winning the FA Cup in 1933, must have given him huge pleasure and satisfaction as he looked back on how far the club had come since his early playing days with St Domingo's.

PROGRESS ON THE FIELD

Solid foundations were laid in the 1879/80 season, the first as Everton, and performances had been sufficiently impressive for the club to decide to apply for membership of the newly formed Lancashire Football Association before the start of the 1880/81 season. Their application was accepted, and with membership of the Association came the opportunity to take part in cup competition for the first time. Friendlies were the staple football diet of the day, and they were often frustrating for players and spectators alike. Apart from lacking the excitement and competitive edge of cup ties, many of them were so one-sided that they were not worth watching. Furthermore, games were often cancelled with a minimum of notice or none at all, kick-off times and the length of games were frequently altered on the day without notice, teams sometimes turned up with a shortage of players and had to recruit spectators, and on occasions a team did not turn up for a game at all because they had found more attractive opposition elsewhere. It is hardly surprising, then, that cup games provided the greatest form of excitement until the introduction of the Football League in 1888.

However, Everton's first experience of cup football proved to be quite traumatic. Following an encouraging 1-1 draw away from home in the first round against Great Lever, they were mauled 8-1 in the replay at Stanley Park. Their confidence could have been shattered, but it was a measure of their growing stature that they were able to take this humiliation in their stride and redeem the season with excellent results in the 17 friendly matches played. Of these, they won 15, drew one and lost one. They kept a clean sheet in 11 matches.

With such good results behind them, it was time to take the club further forward. As an indication of a more professional outlook, the decision was taken to change the strip for the start of the 1881/82 season. The team was still playing in a variety of jerseys of different colours. Apart from looking ridiculous, it wasn't likely to help forge a clear sense of identity. However, new strips were expensive and, in an era of no sponsors, beyond the club's reach. One of the players hit on the ingenious idea of dyeing the existing jerseys black and placing a scarlet sash diagonally across them by way of contrast. The new colours earned the team the nickname the 'Black Watch' after the famous Royal Highland Regiment of that name. In later years, salmon pink and ruby red were experimented with, but it was not until the 1901/02 season that the famous royal blue shirts and white shorts first made their appearance.

The change of strip represented a new outlook but its significance was as nothing compared with the seismic shift the club was about to experience in the management of its affairs. Overlooking their pitch in Stanley Park stood (and still stands) an imposing red-brick building called Stanley House. Its presence could not have been more symbolic. It was the home of local brewer, John Houlding, who was destined to become one of the most powerful figures in Liverpool politics and a colossus in the history of the city's two great football clubs. Just before the start of the 1881/82 season, he was appointed president of Everton FC. The football landscape of Liverpool – and England – was about to change forever.

CHAPTER 3
JOHN HOULDING AND THE ROAD TO ANFIELD

In whatever sphere John Houlding became involved, he was a success. He possessed enormous drive, unlimited energy and consuming ambition combined with a natural instinct for politics and a shrewd business sense. As a councillor he earned the nickname 'King John of Everton' for his dominance of local politics before becoming Lord Mayor of Liverpool. He established a thriving brewery business and owned five public houses. And he was the architect of both Everton's and Liverpool's meteoric rise to the very pinnacle of English football. For a person who was to achieve so much, John Houlding could not have had a less promising start in life.

He was born in 1833 in Liverpool at 15 Tenterden Street, just off Scotland Road. Coincidentally, this was very close to Alfred Riley Wade's birthplace in Eldon Street. The area had not yet been completely overrun by rows of terraced houses and there was still sufficient countryside close at hand for John's father, Thomas, to keep cows and make a living selling milk. John and his brother, William, two years his junior, would often lend their father a hand.

John's formal education began at the Church of England North Free School in nearby Bond Street before transferring to Liverpool College in Shaw Street. He left school at the age of 11 to start work as an errand boy in the Custom House but did not stay long as his father needed help with the family milk business. However, this collapsed when cattle plague struck the district and John, William and their father were forced to look for work elsewhere. John found employment as a drayman at Clarkson's Brewery in Soho Street delivering beer. However, he greatly impressed his employer by his hard work and conscientious attitude, and was rewarded with promotion to foreman and then, at the age of only 20, chief brewer.

He thoroughly enjoyed the work, and after gaining appropriate experience he decided to save up and start his own business. His first venture was the acquisition of a public house, but by shrewd business sense and sheer hard work he was able, by the age of 31, to establish his own brewery in Tynemouth Street. He never looked back. His Houlding's Sparkling Ales were a runaway success and made his name in the world of business. With profits from the brewery he was able to buy Stanley House, a grand residence in Anfield Road overlooking Stanley Park, for himself, his wife Jane and their two children, Alice and William. Houlding had arrived.

However, Houlding's interests did not remain narrowly confined to business. He was a man of many parts. Despite the many demands on his time in running a flourishing brewery, he never forgot those less fortunate than himself. He had particular compassion for the destitute and first launched himself into charity work in 1869 when he helped provide a Christmas dinner in a schoolroom in West Derby Road for the elderly poor of the district. Although there were only 18 recipients that year, the number eventually rose to 1,000.

Houlding's home:
Stanley House in Anfield
Road – from the gate
you can see Anfield

Above: Houlding pictured in 1893

Right: View from the entrance of Houlding's front gate towards Anfield stadium

Houlding became even more involved in charity work for the poor when he was elected in 1873 to the Board of Guardians of the West Derby Union, the body responsible for running a group of local workhouses. The workhouse was the last refuge for those who had no means of supporting themselves and faced starvation. Here they were given food and shelter in return for their labour (hence the name 'workhouse'). The poor were originally the responsibility of individual church parishes and received support (parish relief) at home, but in 1834 a new government act forced them to live in workhouses run by unions – parishes that clubbed together to pool their resources.

Houlding was also concerned for the welfare of orphans and played a prominent part in establishing an orphanage for 650 children run by the West Derby Union. This was the Cottage Homes for Children built in Fazakerley in 1888/89. When Houlding opened the new swimming pool at the orphanage in 1890 he was not afraid to show a human touch: he happily discarded his formal clothing in favour of a bathing costume and took a dip himself.

In 1887 he was elected chairman of the West Derby Union, then the largest union of workhouses in England. His efficiency and organisational ability in running the establishment so impressed his fellow guardians that he was elected chairman twice, the only person to receive this honour. And he was further honoured by his colleagues when a specially commissioned painting of himself was hung in the boardroom of the offices at Brougham Terrace. When he died in 1902 at the age of 69, he was the oldest member of the West Derby Board of Guardians. He had served the organisation faithfully for almost 30 years.

His involvement with the West Derby Union had led to him becoming a prominent member of the North-Western Poor Law Conference, the umbrella organisation that oversaw the workhouses of Lancashire and Cheshire. He was a regular speaker at its annual gatherings, making a considerable impact with his frank and direct views.

When the Stanley Hospital for the treatment of chest diseases was opened in Kirkdale in 1867, Houlding immediately became one of its greatest supporters. He threw himself wholeheartedly into fundraising, organising numerous fairs and galas. When president of Everton FC, he also arranged special charity matches for the benefit of the hospital. As a token of gratitude for his support, he was presented with a silver punch bowl in 1893.

It was inevitable that his social conscience would eventually lead him into politics. He became a member of the Conservative Party, possibly because he found it difficult to align himself with the ruling Liberal Party's anti-drink

ethos. As a brewer he would not have welcomed the legislation introduced by the Liberals in 1872 restricting the opening hours of public houses.

In 1884 he was elected to represent Everton and Kirkdale, the largest municipal ward in the UK with its 26,000 voters. Houlding took the seat with a majority of 2,379 and duly entered the City Council on 21 November 1884. 'Thus commenced a career of great usefulness on behalf of his native city', stated the *Liverpool Mercury* of 18 March 1902. In fact, Houlding was to enjoy such influence and popularity in the district that he acquired the nickname 'King John of Everton'. 'King John' represented the Everton and Kirkdale ward for 11 years until it was absorbed into new wards following the extension of the city's boundaries on 5 September 1895. He then became a member of the bench of aldermen, the city's governing body.

As an alderman, Houlding devoted considerable time and energy trying to improve sanitation and hygiene in Liverpool. He was concerned that the city's refuse was disposed of at sea or deposited untreated in suburban tips. After close investigation of alternative methods, he introduced the use of 'destructors', a substantially more hygienic and efficient process. His concern for health matters regularly took him to major conferences, including the annual congress of the British Institute of Public Health. Such was his standing in this field that he was invited at the 1896 gathering in Glasgow to contribute a paper entitled 'The History of the Treatment and Disposal of City Refuse in Liverpool During the Last Fifty Years'. He was prepared to travel long distances to further his knowledge, even attending a sanitary congress in Moscow in 1897 as a representative of the city.

With regard to health, Houlding believed in the benefits of fresh air, and worked hard to provide more open spaces for the city's inhabitants. To this end he served as deputy chairman of the Parks Committee and as a member of the Acquisition of Land for Open Spaces Sub-Committee.

In 1897 he was made a Justice of the Peace but he was to receive an even greater distinction that year. His outstanding service to the city and the council were duly recognised when he was elected Lord Mayor in November 1897, an honour that meant a great deal to him. However, he did not enjoy a completely smooth ride in attaining this high office. The fact that he was a brewer was not viewed favourably in many quarters, and vociferous voices were raised in protest at his selection. The fact that he met with considerable opposition is not surprising when it is remembered that the Temperance Movement was still strong at that time.

In terms of religious affiliation, Houlding was a member of the Church of England. He attended St Saviour's in Everton but later worshipped at the church of St Simon and St Jude in Anfield Road only a short distance from

his home. He was also a member of the Orange Order, the organisation that originated in Ireland pledging to uphold Protestantism. However, his deepest affinity was with the Freemasons and he was, in fact, one of the first representatives of Freemasonry in Liverpool. He was also one of its most enthusiastic and influential adherents. In 1897, the year he served as Lord Mayor, he was granted the title of Grand Senior Deacon of England. With this position came the privilege of sitting on the right of the Prince of Wales (later Edward VII), the Grand Master of the Order of England.

Houlding was a great lover of learning and appropriately became a member of the Council of University College (now the University of Liverpool). He had a particular passion for literature and was also a very able French scholar. But it was in sport that he found his main recreational pleasures, being a very active swimmer and cricketer. In his younger days he played for Breckfield Cricket Club. He also took a great interest in quoits, becoming president in 1868 of the Everton Quoits Club, which was based at the Cabbage Hall Hotel in Anfield Road, conveniently near his home. However, it is with football that his name will forever be linked. When he became president of Everton FC in 1881 it marked the beginning of an association with that club that was to change football history.

THE MOVE TO PRIORY ROAD

Houlding would have been well satisfied with his first season as president, 1881/82. The club won 15 of its 20 friendly matches and made better progress in the Lancashire Cup than in the previous season. Furthermore, there was a growing interest in the club, with sometimes as many as 2,000 spectators watching their games. But the playing days in Stanley Park were about to end. Towards the close of the 1882/83 season, the Parks Committee refused permission to allow football games to spill over into the cricket season, a ruling that made it impossible for teams such as Everton to complete their fixtures. The only solution was to find another ground.

For Houlding the situation presented not so much a problem as an opportunity. The pitch at Stanley Park was not enclosed, therefore making it impossible to charge an admission fee to watch Everton's matches. And with growing attendances, a very useful source of income was being lost. Houlding had the answer. A short distance across the park in Priory Road stood Coney Green, a house belonging to his friend William Cruitt, a wealthy cattle salesman. Next to the house was a large field which was ideal for a football pitch. Houlding approached Cruitt and without great difficulty secured permission from him to rent the field, fence it off and erect a small stand and dressing room.

Work duly went ahead during the summer of 1883 in preparation for the start of the new season. And what a great season it was. Not only were

Gone but not forgotten: This garage stands on the site of Everton's second ground. It was a field in Priory Road next to Coney Green, the name of the house owned by William Cruitt. Cruitt was a cattle salesman and friend of John Houlding

Everton unbeaten in 14 of their 16 friendly matches but they also secured their first trophy, the Liverpool Cup. Things were looking very good, but there was a black cloud on the horizon. Cruitt, dismayed by the volume of noise that intruded into his home on matchdays, decided before the end of the season that enough was enough. Income from rent could not compensate for the loss of peace and quiet he had to endure. Everton were told to move on.

THE MOVE TO ANFIELD

Houlding once again stepped into the breach. He was well connected, and this time approached a fellow brewer, Joseph Orrell, for help. Orrell owned land in Walton Breck Road that was lying idle, and Houlding asked if Everton could rent it. Orrell readily agreed but insisted on the following arrangement: 'That we, the Everton Football Club, keep the existing walls in good repair, pay the taxes, do not cause ourselves to be a nuisance to Mr Orrell and other tenants adjoining, and also pay a small sum as rent, or subscribe a donation each year to the Stanley Hospital in the name of Mr Orrell.' The terms were accepted and Houlding was duly appointed the club's representative tenant, paying rent in his own name for the hire of the field.

Once again, as at Priory Road, hard work was called for to transform the field into a football ground. The club members set about the task enthusiastically and managed to fence off the pitch, erect a stand and fix hoardings to the walls in time for the start of the 1884/85 season. The end product may not have looked a work of art but it met the club's requirements. However, what these youthful Everton enthusiasts could not have known was the significance of their achievement. They had, in fact, just made history. Ironically, the humble ground they had just built was to become world-renowned as Anfield – the home of Liverpool FC!

CHAPTER 4
EVERTON AT ANFIELD —
CHAMPIONS OF ENGLAND

THE DEPARTURE OF BEN CHAMBERS FROM ST DOMINGO'S

There were great days ahead for Everton at their new Anfield ground, but before examining these, it would be good to remind ourselves that there would have been no Everton FC at all unless the Reverend Ben Swift Chambers had set the ball rolling that led to the club's birth. So what became of this important figure in the club's history?

After five years in Liverpool, Chambers' period of service at St Domingo's came to an end in 1882 when he was appointed superintendent minister of the Southport circuit. In his five years at the chapel he had made many close friends and become a very popular minister. His three daughters were also born during his time there: first Maud in 1878, then Minnie in 1879 and finally Dora in 1881. All three were baptised at St Domingo's. Chambers would have had very fond memories of Liverpool and doubtlessly it would have been a great wrench for him to leave.

Something of the impression he had made can be gauged from the minutes of the St Domingo's Leaders' Meeting of 8 June 1882, which pay tribute to the 'faithful and diligent discharge of the duties which have devolved upon him as superintendent minister of the Liverpool circuit during the past five years' and 'the kind, courteous and impartial manner which he has displayed when presiding over the meetings connected with this church'. His wife, Elizabeth, had also made a great impression, and the minutes make specific mention of the 'kindly influence' she exercised at the chapel.

Undoubtedly the Chambers family would be greatly missed, but their story does not finish here. They were to return to St Domingo's for a further four years from 1890 to 1894 when Ben was appointed minister and circuit superintendent for a second time. But little did he know that his return was to coincide with one of the most turbulent periods in Merseyside's football history and that his organist, George Mahon, would be involved in an upheaval at Everton Football Club of almost seismic proportions...

EVERTON'S FIRST SEASON AT ANFIELD

27 September 1884 is a date of huge significance in the history of Merseyside football — it was the very first time the world-renowned Anfield stadium staged a football match. Appropriately, in view of the countless glorious triumphs and honours this stadium was to witness in the course of the next 125 years, the occasion was marked by an exciting 5-0 victory for Everton in their game against Earlestown. For the record, the team that day, playing in a 2-2-6 formation, was: Lindsay; Marriott, Morris; Pickering, Preston; Richards, Parry, Gibson, Whittle, McGill, Higgins. Michael Higgins goes down in history as the first goalscorer at Anfield.

Champions: The first Everton team to win the league championship, in 1890/91

Back row (left to right): D Waugh (trainer), R Stockton (umpire), A Hannah (captain), J Angus, D Doyle, R Molyneux (secretary)
Middle row (l-r): A Latta, D Kirkwood, J Holt, W Campbell, A Millward
Front row: (l-r): A Brady, F Geary, E Chadwick

Nerve centre: The Sandon
Hotel, with Anfield looming
large in the background

was ideally located to offer this facility. It made perfect sense to make the switch. This duly went ahead, and almost immediately the hostelry became the venue for all committee meetings and the hub of all social activities. In addition, the clubhouse of The Sandon's bowling green became the backcloth for most team photographs. As this public house was to play a huge part not only in Everton's but also Liverpool's history – a fact proudly displayed on a memorial mirror inside the building today – it might be interesting to know why Houlding gave it its name.

As already explained, Houlding was a very active member of the Conservative Party. In the course of his political activities he came to know and admire Viscount Sandon, the Conservative MP for Liverpool from 1868 to 1882. Viscount Sandon's actual name was Dudley Ryder and he was a member of the hugely influential Ryder family who originate from Harrowby Hall in Lincolnshire. The family has played a prominent part in British political and social life ever since Nathaniel Ryder was named Baron Harrowby in 1776. That same year he bought the Sandon estate near Stafford, which has remained the family seat ever since. The photograph of Sandon Hall opposite gives some idea of the Ryders' standing in society during the past 200 years or so.

The family's status and prestige were secured in 1809 when Nathaniel's eldest son Dudley (one of several Ryders with this forename) was granted the twin titles of Viscount Sandon and Earl of Harrowby in recognition of his service as foreign secretary. From that date until the present, it has been customary for the Earl of Harrowby's eldest son and heir to be known as Viscount Sandon until the viscount becomes earl himself. The particular Dudley Ryder that Houlding so admired was the third Earl of Harrowby, known as Viscount Sandon until his father's death in 1882.

This Viscount Sandon, as well as being MP for Liverpool, also held important positions in the government. He became President of the Board of Trade in 1878, but perhaps his greatest achievement was the passing of the 1876 Elementary Education Act, which made education compulsory for children up to the age of 10. From that time it became illegal to employ them in factories, mills or anywhere else beneath the age of 10.

Houlding, already a successful and wealthy brewer and owner of five public houses, extended his business activities in the drinks trade further by opening a new public house on Oldfield Road in 1881. He named it The Sandon Hotel in honour of Viscount Sandon for whom he had such high regard. And that same year the viscount became a patron of Everton FC. He appears in the club records as 'Lord Sandon' in 1881 and 1882 but as 'The Earl of Harrowby' from 1883 on inheriting his father's title. It would be interesting to know if the occupants of Sandon Hall, the magnificent stately home in Staffordshire, are aware of their link with Everton and Liverpool's history.

Everton's results that historic first season at Anfield were more than respectable in view of the increasingly formidable opposition they met. Of the 23 matches played there, 14 were victories, two were draws and seven were defeats. It gives some indication of the club's growing reputation that two recent winners of the FA Cup, Blackburn Olympic and Blackburn Rovers, were willing to play them. The season was also marked by another appearance in the Liverpool Cup final, although, sadly, there was to be no trophy this time. Nevertheless, Everton were becoming a force to be reckoned with, and it would not be too long before John Houlding saw an opportunity to step up a gear to maximise the club's commercial potential. Important changes were afoot.

THE SANDON

Houlding had already begun to secure a firm hold on Everton when he made his public house, The Sandon Hotel, the club's nerve centre as soon as the Anfield ground was complete. He had the perfect excuse for moving the headquarters there. The new ground had no dressing rooms and The Queen's Head was too far away to be of any use on matchdays. The Sandon, on the other hand, stood almost in the shadow of the ground and

The original Sandon: Viscount Sandon aka Dudley Ryder, third Earl of Harrowby and MP for Liverpool 1868-1882, and his family's home in Stafford – Sandon Hall

EVERTON – CHAMPIONS OF ENGLAND

Houlding saw the opportunity to take Everton another step forward when The Football Association, the game's governing body, legalised professionalism in 1885. Until that year, football had been officially a wholly amateur sport, although The FA recognised that professionalism did exist in various illegal guises. Acting on sound commercial instincts, Houlding seized the opportunity to embrace professionalism and strengthen the squad by signing better players. A more attractive team meant bigger gates, and even though Everton were attracting up to 10,000 spectators for some games, Houlding wanted to improve on this. He promptly signed the club's first three professionals in time for the start of the 1885/86 season: George Dobson from Bolton Wanderers, George Farmer from Oswestry and Alec Dick from Kilmarnock in Scotland.

Even with a strengthened squad, Everton got off to a bad start as a professional club, winning only one of their first seven matches. However, 22 wins and three draws in the remaining 32 games, as well as lifting the Liverpool Cup, fully redeemed the season. The following season again saw the Liverpool Cup in Everton's hands and, assured of the club's progress, Houlding was convinced he had a strong enough team to apply for membership of the Football League when it was created in the 1888/89 season. The purpose of the league was to provide the top 12 professional clubs in England with a programme of regular competitive matches instead of the present unsatisfactory diet of friendlies and occasional cup ties. Not everyone shared Houlding's assessment of Everton's abilities, and there was great surprise when the club was elected to join the elite dozen in place of others that were considered to be significantly stronger. It was widely believed that Everton were the weakest of the 12 clubs elected, and that they would therefore struggle in the new league.

One of the clubs left out in the cold was Bootle, considered to be the strongest on Merseyside and more deserving of a place than Everton. William McGregor, founder of the Football League, readily admitted that, while some of the excluded clubs had better playing records than those selected, they could not compete with them in terms of gates. This led to a storm of protest in the press. 'Here we have it in one word,' complained James Catton (the famous correspondent of *Athletic News* who wrote under the name of 'Tityrus'). 'The whole thing is a mere money-making scheme, a speculation.' Further criticism appeared in a Birmingham newspaper on 21 April: 'The League, as at present constituted, is not formed for the purpose of encouraging football. It is formed so that the allied clubs may make more money than they already do.'

Whatever the criticisms, Everton duly took their place in the Football League. But it was not a season to remember. They partially fulfilled the prophecies of those who scoffed at their ability by finishing eighth out of 12 clubs. And in addition, for some unknown reason, they chose not to enter any cup competitions. But their inglorious debut was quickly forgotten when they secured the runners-up spot the following season, finishing only two points behind Preston North End. And only a year later, at the end of the 1890/91 season, they finally silenced their critics when they achieved their first taste of real glory. The club that many predicted would sink in the Football League had just become its champions.

Fighter: George Mahon stood
up against John Houlding,
causing the split at Anfield

CHAPTER 5
HOULDING, MAHON AND THE BATTLE OF ANFIELD

Everton had snatched the title by a mere two points from mighty Preston North End, the club whose dominance of the Football League in the competition's inaugural season, coupled with an unstoppable run in the FA Cup (they lifted the trophy without conceding a single goal), had earned them the nickname 'The Invincibles'. To no one's surprise, Preston again won the championship the following season even though they were pushed hard all the way by Everton. But it was the men from Anfield who finally burst their bubble in 1890/91 and deprived them of a hat-trick of league titles.

What a season that was for Everton's faithful legion of supporters. In only three years they had watched their team progress from being so-called 'no-hopers' to champions of the Football League. No wonder there was reason to celebrate. And celebrate they did, even after a 1-0 defeat in the last home match of the season against – who else? – Preston. When the final whistle blew, they carried the Everton players shoulder-high back from Anfield to the dressing rooms at The Sandon in triumphal procession. This was a day they were going to enjoy.

It is hard to believe that only 13 years previously the new champions of the Football League were just a humble chapel side playing in a local park. Their meteoric rise had been largely due to the vision and drive of John Houlding. Houlding had not only given the club a clear sense of purpose and direction, but had also given it considerable financial support out of his own pocket. The minutes of the management committee meeting of 5 October 1891 record that he had advanced £180 in 1886/87, £350 in 1887/88, £1,200 in 1888/89 and £600 in 1889/90. Those were very large sums of money at that time. Not surprisingly, perhaps, he felt that he was entitled to something in return for his investment. And so began a chain of events that was to have momentous consequences.

THE GROWING RIFT WITH HOULDING

Houlding, as the club's representative tenant, had been paying rent in his own name to John Orrell for hire of the field on which the Anfield stadium was built. He then sub-let the ground to Everton as their landlord. Not unmindful of the many financial sacrifices he had made on the club's behalf, and, conscious of the club's growing prosperity from gate receipts, he felt it would be reasonable to use his powers as landlord to change the terms of the original rental agreement in his favour. He therefore cancelled the existing fixed-rate terms and began to charge rent in proportion to increase in income. This occurred in two stages. Having fixed a rate of £100 in the 1885/86 season, Houlding raised it to £240 at the start of the 1888/89 season when Everton became members of the Football League, and to £250 at the start of the 1890/91 season.

The rent issue, though very important, was only part of the reason for the growing tension between Houlding and other members of the management committee. For one thing, there was considerable ill-feeling

Mahon's gravestone: He died in 1908, but his legacy lives on

about the use of licensed premises as the club's headquarters. There was still a strong St Domingo presence among the club's members, and The Sandon did not sit comfortably with their temperance beliefs. Nor were they happy at Houlding's insistence that the only refreshments on sale at the ground should be his own ale.

But the real crunch came at the committee meeting of 15 September 1891 when Houlding's letter containing the following extract was read out:

'I am compelled to give you notice which I hereby do that you must give up possession of the piece of land situated between Anfield Rd and Walton Breck Road used as a football ground with the approaches thereto after the close of the present season viz April 30th 1892.'

His reason was that Orrell, owner of the field on which the stadium stood, wanted to use the land for other purposes. Houlding himself had bought land next to Orrell's and saw this as the ideal opportunity to present the club with a prospectus proposing that Everton should become a limited company and buy his land and Orrell's for £8,737.10s.

Everton at Anfield: The main stand in 1891, prior to Everton's move to Goodison Park

'The site is well known to residents and football visitors to Liverpool, and is admitted to be a most valuable position for a football club to occupy. The enormous number of spectators who witness the various matches on the ground testify to this.'

It stresses the advantage that Houlding's and Orrell's land combined 'will together make one of the finest football grounds in the United Kingdom', and would also enable the new limited company 'to add cycling and running tracks, so that the company's ground can be used for athletic sports all the year round'. These would generate a valuable source of additional income.

GEORGE MAHON ENTERS THE FRAY

The resolution was proposed and seconded, but before things could be taken any further, a bearded figure leapt boldly to his feet and opposed the scheme. It was George Mahon, an articulate and persuasive speaker who was not convinced Houlding really did have the best interests of the club at heart. The prospectus was stopped dead in its tracks. The Battle of Anfield had begun.

Houlding's motives have been questioned ever since. Some believe he wanted to take the club forward by helping it acquire land suitable for increasing the ground's capacity and expanding its facilities as success continued. However, the feeling among most club members at the time was that this was a blatant case of profiteering, as Houlding's share of the sale would yield him a substantial profit. A visionary or an opportunist? Perhaps he was both. We shall probably never really know. Whatever the perceptions of himself, he was confident his prospectus would have an easy passage through the committee. After all, it seemed to present compelling logic:

Houlding was confronted with an opponent of considerable stature. Mahon, the senior partner in Roose, Mahon and Howard, a leading accountancy firm in North John Street, was one of the most respected men in Liverpool. Born on 27 July 1853 at 12 Birkett Street, he was the son of Robert Mahon, a shoemaker. The family left Liverpool for Dublin while George was a child, but it seems they returned when Robert changed occupations to become a bookkeeper. By the age of 22, George Mahon was working as a cashier and living at 108 Field Street. It was from here that he married Margaret Fyffe, a joiner's daughter, at St Peter's Church in Everton on 31 August 1875. They were to have three daughters and two sons.

Perhaps because his early years were spent in Ireland where Association football had yet to take hold, Mahon showed little interest in the game until a friend, Sam Crosbie, a leading light in Liverpool's educational and musical circles, took him to watch Everton play Preston North End in 1887. Mahon was hooked by what he saw, and from that point on there was no stopping him. Football became a consuming passion, and two years later, aged 36, he was elected to the Everton management committee.

Among Mahon's other interests was a deep involvement with St Domingo's. He established a close working relationship with the Reverend Ben Chambers, who had returned to the chapel as minister in 1890 after an eight-year absence. It didn't take Chambers long to recognise Mahon's talent as an organist, and when the chapel organist resigned in September 1890 Chambers wasted no time in asking Mahon to step into the breach. It was quite an honour to be offered the position. Music was of central importance in the chapel's worship, and the selection of an organist was normally a quite rigorous procedure. Mahon expressed a willingness to help, but despite Chambers' best efforts to persuade him to take the position permanently, Mahon insisted he would only hold the fort on a temporary basis. In fact, he stayed on until October 1891, much longer than he probably would have liked. It took well over a year to find someone of the right calibre to take over from him.

It would have been quite unreasonable to expect Mahon to fill the role permanently. His accountancy work was time-consuming enough and he would not have been able to put in the many hours required for choir practice, church functions and special occasions. But much more significantly, he had become embroiled in events unfolding at Anfield that would not only make huge demands on his time but also drain him physically and emotionally, especially as he did not enjoy good health. As former Everton director Tom Keates states in his history of the club in 1928:

'The "split" involved a considerable sacrifice of time by the revolutionists, mental anxiety, diversion from their urgent business responsibilities, monetary risks, partisan denunciation, and misrepresentation.'

The pressures to which Mahon was subjected at this period may well have contributed to his early death at the age of 55 on 9 December 1908, tragically just one week after his 25-year-old son Herbert.

THE SPLIT

Whatever his physical frailties, Mahon was a man of indomitable spirit, and he threw himself wholeheartedly and energetically into the fight with Houlding. He was not prepared to meet the increased rent demands or to purchase Anfield on what he considered to be inflated terms. It was time to make a stand. Mahon called a special general meeting at Liverpool College in Shaw Street on 25 January 1892.

At the meeting Mahon delivered an impassioned speech against Houlding's prospectus with such conviction and eloquence that all but 18 of the assembled 500 club members were swept along by the force of his arguments. The minutes of the meeting record: 'That we do not entertain Mr Houlding's proposal to form the club into a limited liability in accordance with Mr Houlding's prospectus.'

Despite the massive gulf that was opening up between Houlding and the committee, it was agreed at the meeting that there should be one last attempt to bring about a compromise. The minutes state clearly the terms on which this could be reached. It was proposed:

'That we offer Mr Houlding £180 per annum for the ground used by the Everton Football Club on lease for 10 years, rent to be paid quarterly in advance. The Tenants to have the option of purchase of the land at 7/6 per yard, such purchase to be arranged between now and April 30th 94. All fixtures to be the property of the Club. Mr Houlding not to have the right of a nominee on the Committee. This offer to remain open for seven days: failing Mr Houlding's acceptance that the Committee do lease one of the other grounds on terms of Committee's report.'

Anticipating that Houlding would never agree to these terms, Mahon had already astutely pre-empted the inevitable expulsion from Anfield by looking for another ground. He had found a field across Stanley Park at Mere Green Field adjoining Goodison Road and was convinced this was the right location. However, anyone who saw it could have been forgiven for thinking he must have been barking mad. It was aptly described in a 1905 Everton match programme as having 'degenerated from meadow land into a howling desert'. Anything less likely to serve as a football ground would have been difficult to imagine. Despite its bleak appearance, Mahon

fully believed in its potential and was determined that Everton should secure a lease on it. When he suggested to the meeting that the club should consider an alternative ground to Anfield, he was sarcastically dismissed by a Houlding supporter with the taunt: 'Yer can't find one!' Mahon instantly played his trump card, proclaiming triumphantly: 'I've got one in my pocket!'

Predictably, perhaps, there was no reply from Houlding to Mahon's terms. This was clearly the point of no return, and the parting of the ways was officially confirmed in the words of the following club minutes of 8 February 1892:

> *'Proposed that as we have not received Mr Houldings acceptance of the Clubs offer of £180 per annum for the Ground and as Mr Houlding had given the Club notice to quit the present ground, the Clubs solicitors be instructed to arrange for a lease of the Goodison Road Ground. [original punctuation]'*

And the end of King John's reign was finally proclaimed at the general meeting of 15 March 1892 when the resolution was carried by a large majority:

Marking 100 years since Mahon's death: Peter Lupson (second right) with Mahon's descendants Emma Murphy (great-great-granddaughter), Graham Murphy (great-grandson), Alan Bell (great-grandson) and Jim Garner (great-grandson) at Goodison

Left: The George Mahon Cup, which was instituted in his memory not long after his death and is still played for today

> *'That Messrs John Houlding, Alexander Nisbet, and Thomas C Howarth, having lost the confidence of the Members of the Club, be respectively removed from the Presidency and Committee.'*

Things would never be the same again.

CHAPTER 6
MIGRATION TO GOODISON PARK – AND THE BIRTH OF LIVERPOOL FC

HOULDING FORMS LIVERPOOL FOOTBALL CLUB

Mahon and the majority of the Everton committee were now officially homeless, but before turning their attention to securing and developing Mere Green Field there was still another important battle to be fought.

Houlding, undaunted by the fact that only a rump of the committee and just three players had remained loyal to him, pressed ahead with his plans to form a limited liability company and duly registered 'The Everton Football Club and Athletic Ground Company Limited' at Somerset House. But once again it was George Mahon who was his stumbling block. Learning of Houlding's action, Mahon immediately appealed to The Football Association, the game's ruling body, claiming that the name 'Everton' was already in use. He insisted that the substantial majority of the management committee, although expelled from Anfield, remained the rightful custodians of the club and its name.

The FA Council met to debate the issue. There must have been considerable tension for both parties as they awaited the verdict. In the end it proved to be another setback for Houlding. After careful deliberation, The FA ruled in Mahon's favour, stating that "The Council will not accept any membership of any club bearing a name similar to one affiliated with this Association in the name of the Everton club".

Houlding was no doubt bitterly disappointed with The FA's decision, but he did not swerve from his intention to run a club at Anfield. If all he needed was a new name, he would find one. It was his close friend, William Barclay, his vice-president at Everton, who came up with the inspired idea of choosing one that would have city-wide appeal and thereby attract more supporters. At a meeting in Houlding's house he proposed 'Liverpool Football Club'. It was instantly approved.

However, things never seemed to run smoothly for Houlding, and he once again encountered opposition. This time it came from a rugby club in the city that already bore that name. But the difficulty was soon overcome when it was suggested that the addition of a single word in the title of Houlding's club would distinguish it from the rugby club. And so, in May 1892, 'The Liverpool Association Football Club' was formally registered.

DR BAXTER SECURES GOODISON PARK

Meanwhile, Everton had the formidable task of turning Mere Green Field into a proper football ground in time for the start of the 1892/93 season. Time was limited and building costs were worryingly high. Most of the money could be raised from shares, savings and compensation for the fittings left behind at Anfield, but there was still a crucial shortfall that threatened to jeopardise the entire project. Things would undoubtedly have ground to an immediate halt but for the intervention of one of their directors, Dr James Clement Baxter. Concerned at the club's desperate

Humble beginnings: Houlding (front row, centre) with his Liverpool team in 1893

Park life: Loans from Dr James Clement Baxter (right) made the construction of Goodison Park (left) possible. It was opened by Lord Kinnaird, president of the FA (above) on 27 Aug 1892

plight, Baxter unhesitatingly offered a loan of £1,000 – a very considerable sum at that time – interest-free and without security. It was a magnanimous gesture and it secured Goodison Park as the new home base. For this act of generosity alone, Baxter was certain of his place in Everton's history, but his service to the club extended far beyond this. It is worth knowing more about this remarkable man.

James Clement Baxter was the son of chemist William Baxter and was born at Great Homer Street, Liverpool, in 1857. After his education at St Francis Xavier College, a respected Roman Catholic school in the city, he proceeded to the King and Queen's College of Physicians of Ireland in Dublin to train as a doctor. On graduation he returned to Liverpool to practise with his uncle in Great Homer Street before eventually setting up on his own in Robson Street, Everton.

Baxter's care for his patients, most of whom were from poor Catholic families, became legendary. He had literally hundreds on his books and he worked long hours tending to their needs. He soon became known as one of the busiest men in Liverpool. Such was his dedication that when he became too ill to walk to his surgery at the very end of his life, he insisted on being helped there. But his work as a doctor extended beyond Robson Street. He was medical officer at Beacon Lane Orphanage for 30 years, and he served as doctor to St Edward's College for many years. (At that time it was a seminary for the training of Roman Catholic priests, although it later became a respected Catholic boys' school.) Baxter's sound medical knowledge was also much in demand

from insurance companies who trusted his judgements implicitly.

One of his chief qualities of character was remarkable generosity with money. As well as tending to the medical needs of the poor, he also gave liberally from his own pocket to make their lives easier. As a director of Everton he also worked hard to ensure that players felt properly valued. When The Football Association introduced the maximum wage of £4 per week in 1900, Everton, like most clubs, chose to pay this amount only to their very best players. Baxter became increasingly unhappy with this state of affairs. He felt strongly that all members of the first team should be treated equally. After all, they had to pull together on the pitch and work as one if they were to achieve a result. He made this an issue at the management committee meeting of 1 December 1903. As the following minutes record, he managed to persuade his fellow directors that equal pay was the right policy for the club:

'Dr Baxter proposed and after discussion it was resolved that, as an experiment and in order to further stimulate the enthusiasm of the younger players if possible, a uniform maximum wage of four pounds should be paid to the eleven players who shall actually play in the remaining League matches and English Cup ties.'

Although Baxter was fully aware that this would increase the weekly wages bill, he felt that good morale among the players was a much more important consideration.

Baxter gave loyal and devoted service to Everton from the moment he was elected to the board of directors in 1889 until his death 39 years later in 1928. In the course of those 39 years he served as director, chairman and even club doctor. As Everton chairman, Baxter was respected for his tact and control at committee meetings. Even in the most heated debates his tranquil spirit had a calming effect on those present, and he could easily bring a meeting to order in a quiet, unostentatious manner. He also had the advantage of great charm and a sunny smile.

His love for football was boundless, not merely confined to the professional game. He gave much encouragement and support to junior clubs and was actively involved with several as president or patron.

Baxter rarely took holidays, being content to travel with the Everton team to away matches or to travel to meetings of the Football Association and the Football League. He did, however, have a love for the cinema, even to the extent of some business involvement.

In addition to his medical work and his involvement with Everton, Baxter

also took an active part in local politics. In 1906 he was elected Liberal councillor for the St Anne's ward, serving there until 1920. His main concerns as a member of the City Council were housing, energy and public transport, and he sat on committees relating to these. Possibly his interest in public transport stemmed from his dissatisfaction with the inadequate tram services provided on matchdays for the thousands of Everton and Liverpool supporters travelling to Goodison or Anfield. The club minutes of 11 August 1903 certainly point to this:

'Resolved that Messrs Baxter, Davies & the Secretary be appointed to act with the L'pool F.C. as a deputation to the Tramways Manager with a view to obtaining a better service of trams on the occasion of our matches.'

After a lifetime of dedicated service to his community, Dr Baxter died at his home 110 Robson Street on 27 January 1928 at the age of 71. A Requiem Mass was said for him at the Church of Our Lady Immaculate in St Domingo Road, followed by interment at Anfield Cemetery. It was a very sad day for his wife Eugenie, their two sons Reginald and Cecil (both doctors), and their daughter Evelyn. The family endowed a stained glass window at the Church of Our Lady Immaculate in his memory and it was unveiled on 1 July 1928. His younger son, Cecil, succeeded him on the board of directors and as club doctor at Everton, serving the club faithfully until his own death in 1954. This represented an unbroken link of 65 years between the family and the club.

It has often been assumed that Dr Baxter's deep faith as a Roman Catholic and his close ties with Catholic organisations are further evidence that Everton is a Catholic club. This is another mistake. It has already been pointed out that the chapel where Everton was born has nothing to do with Catholicism despite the Latin-sounding ring to its name 'St Domingo'. Equally, the presence of a Catholic on the Everton committee should be seen as nothing more than coincidence. Everton remained a predominantly Methodist club with continuing strong ties with St Domingo's. However, Dr Baxter was not made to feel under any pressure from his colleagues at Everton for his Catholic beliefs. The minutes of 13 October 1903 clearly reveal this. When the club arranged a friendly match with Stonyhurst College, the famous Catholic school near Clitheroe in Lancashire, it is recorded that Dr Baxter was invited to pick the Everton team.

THE OPENING OF GOODISON PARK

With money assured by Dr Baxter, work began in earnest in June 1892 in transforming Mere Green Field into a football stadium. It seemed an impossible task to get everything finished in time for the start of the new season but, incredibly, it was achieved. Out of the desolate wasteland arose a stadium considered to be the finest in England. It was named 'Goodison

'Team of Macs':
John McKenna's
first Liverpool team

J. McQue,   J. McCartney,   A. Hannah,   S. H. Ross,   M. McQueen,   D. McLean,   J. McBride   A. Dick (*Trainer*).
T. Wyllie   J. Smith   J. Miller   M. McVean,   H. McQueen

Park' after Goodison Road and was opened on Thursday 27 August 1892 amidst great celebrations. Following a 4pm dinner at the Adelphi Hotel in Liverpool that was presided over by George Mahon, the club's new chairman, the party of dignitaries and invited guests proceeded to Goodison Park in open carriages to attend the formal opening by Lord Kinnaird, president of the Football Association. After the 6pm ceremony, the crowd of some 10,000 were treated to the spectacle of various sports events, a concert by a military band and a firework display. Goodison Park was really opened in style.

The first match at the new ground took place at 5pm on Thursday 1 September 1892. It was a friendly against Bolton Wanderers which Everton won 4-2. The *Liverpool Echo* described the occasion two days later in the following glowing terms:

'After witnessing the enthusiasm displayed on Thursday evening in the match at Goodison Park, few will be bold enough to predict anything else than success for the Everton club... There could not have been less than ten or twelve thousand spectators present when Mr Mahon, the chairman of the club, set the ball rolling for the season, and such a display of enthusiasm has rarely excelled that which was shown when the "champion of the club" stepped into the field of play to give the initial kick. The ground, too, presented a splendid appearance and

nothing but delight was heard expressed at the fine accommodation provided, which gives every person who gains admission an uninterrupted view of the game no matter what part of the field play is going on.'

The Everton team on that historic occasion, playing in a 2-3-5 formation, was: Jardine; Howarth, Dewer; Boyle, Holt, Robertson; Latta, Maxwell, Geary, Chadwick, Milward.

LIVERPOOL KICK OFF

While Everton were playing the mighty Bolton Wanderers amidst great festivities in front of a large crowd, Liverpool Football Club's first-ever match that very same evening was, in total contrast, a very low-key affair. It was a friendly against Rotherham Town of the Midland League, and Anfield was almost deserted, with fewer than 200 spectators in the ground. It was obvious that the overwhelming number of Everton's supporters had not switched allegiance.

Remarkably, every single member of the Liverpool team that day was a Scotsman. New club secretary John McKenna had travelled north of the border in search of talent and recruited 13 players he felt were of the right calibre. Eight of these had typical Scottish surnames beginning with 'Mc' and Liverpool were quickly dubbed 'The Team of Macs'. The team that played

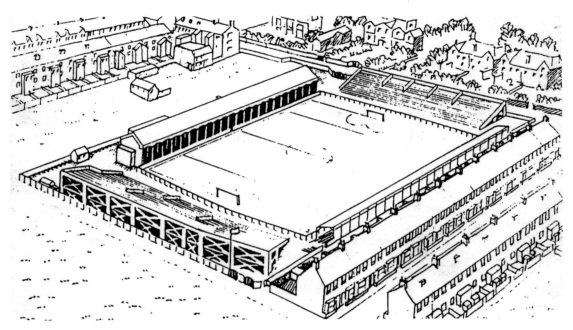

After the split:
Anfield in 1894/95,
showing the first
main stand and
uncovered terracing
behind the goals

Rotherham, and was thus the first to represent Liverpool FC, lined up in a 2-3-5 formation: Ross; Hannah, McLean; Kelso, McQue (not McQueen), McBride; Wyllie, Smith, Miller, McVean, Kelvin.

Just as George Mahon had kicked off the first match at Goodison Park, so Houlding kicked off Liverpool's first match. He was no doubt delighted with the goal rush that followed, Liverpool going into the break with a 5-0 lead. Malcolm McVean has the distinction of going down in history as the scorer of Liverpool's first goal. The home strip that day was blue and white halves and white shorts. It was not until 1896 that the famous red shirts were first worn.

A special match programme costing one old penny was issued for the occasion. It was not a particularly exciting read, containing mostly advertisements and a lengthy explanation of the offside rule in its two sheets of foolscap. There was, however, a very complimentary description of Houlding:

'To know him is to like him, though there are some who are hostile to him. He is a man of energy, determination, and honesty of purpose,

and under his presidency the Liverpool Club is sure to prosper, the same way the Everton Club did.'

Two days later Liverpool played their first match in the Lancashire League, a home encounter against Higher Walton. Their application to join the Football League had been turned down on the grounds that they had yet to establish their credentials as a playing side. Their recent past as Everton did not guarantee continuity of football quality. However, a clear signal that they were heading in the right direction was sent with the 8-0 annihilation of Higher Walton, although once again it was in front of a pitifully low crowd of only 200.

But word was quickly getting around that this was a free-scoring team guaranteed to entertain. By the time of the home match on 24 September interest had grown to such an extent that the attendance leapt to 4,000. The 4-0 victory over Bury that day sent Liverpool to the top of the league and, boosted by their new and enthusiastic following, there was no holding them back. They swept through the Lancashire League, winning 17 of their 22 games, and claimed the championship at the very first attempt. The club's glorious future had just begun.

CHAPTER 7
THE DEATH OF HOULDING – FORGIVENESS AND RECONCILIATION

JOHN MCKENNA, LIVERPOOL'S TRAILBLAZER

The driving force behind Liverpool's rise to football prominence in the early years was John McKenna, the club's first honorary secretary. He was personally appointed to the post by his close friend John Houlding.

McKenna was an Ulsterman born in 1855 in County Monaghan. He was one of thousands of Irish immigrants who came to Liverpool in search of work. Leaving Ireland for Liverpool as a 17-year-old in 1872, he found employment as a grocer's boy running errands and stacking shelves. He later worked as a vaccinations officer for the West Derby Union, the body responsible for the administration of several Liverpool workhouses, but eventually became a prominent businessman.

It was almost inevitable that McKenna and Houlding should meet and become close friends. They shared the same views in politics and religion, and supported the same organisations and causes. They first met at a local lodge of the Orange Order but their friendship deepened through their active involvement with the Freemasons, their membership of the Conservative Party and their work for the West Derby Union. They were also regular worshippers in the Church of England.

McKenna's early sporting interests were rugby and rifle shooting. It was no doubt his love of shooting that motivated him to join the No 5 Battery of the 4th Lancashire Artillery Volunteers. He became a highly respected battery sergeant-major, leaving a lasting impression for both his character and appearance. Just after his death many years later, the following tribute to him appeared on 30 March 1936 in the *Liverpool Post*. It had been written by his former captain, Herbert Southam:

> '*McKenna was a keen disciplinarian, very considerate with the men, and a thorough man of action. His smartness when on parade, sparkling eyes, light red hair, and moustache, remains, even now, to me a portrait of a man I had great fondness for and always respected.*'

The description of McKenna as 'a thorough man of action' perfectly characterised him. Signs of the vision and energy for which he would later become known at Liverpool were already apparent while he was serving with the Volunteers. In 1885, at his initiative, a successful regimental rugby club was formed and McKenna became its chairman. Although Captain Southam did not actually play in the team, he kept a jersey as a fond memento of those days. McKenna's love for rugby did not stop there. He later became actively involved with the West Lancashire Rugby Union.

However, it is with Association football that his name will forever be linked. He became interested in the game when Houlding invited him to watch

Memorial: John Houlding's grave in Everton Cemetery

Liverpool's first honorary
secretary: John McKenna
was appointed by his friend
John Houlding

Everton's matches at Anfield and it wasn't long before rugby lost the hold it had had on him. He became a regular attender at Anfield and was an instantly recognised figure with his bowler hat, velvet-collared overcoat and distinctive moustache with its carefully cultivated points. After the split with Everton, McKenna aligned himself with Houlding's new club, becoming its first secretary. It was the start of a brilliant career in football that would earn him the accolade of 'genius'. Working in tandem with William Barclay, McKenna assumed control of team affairs as secretary-manager while Barclay took care of administrative matters. And McKenna was quickly off the mark. In the club's very first season, his 'Team of Macs', all Scotsmen, gave a clear indication of the good things that lay ahead when they stormed to the title of the Lancashire League.

With this success under his belt, McKenna was hungry for greater things. An advertisement caught his eye inviting clubs to apply for membership of the Second Division of the Football League, and he immediately saw this as Liverpool's golden opportunity to step up to the big time. Without consulting anyone at the club, he sent the following briefly worded telegram to the League secretary: 'Liverpool make application to the Second Division of the League.' But he added the name and address of William Barclay, the club's administrative secretary, not his own. It was an audacious move, as Barclay was opposed to Liverpool joining the Football League.

Things then moved quickly. Barclay received a prompt reply from the League and immediately sent for McKenna, asking him to explain himself. He handed him the telegram he had received which read: 'Liverpool elected. Come to London meeting at 3 o'clock to-morrow to arrange fixtures.' McKenna now had a job on his hands. He had to convince Barclay and the other directors in record time that this was the right move for the club. Remarkably, he not only managed to do so but also persuaded them to let him go to London as the club's official representative. He duly went and returned from the meeting with the season's fixtures in his hand. He had just blazed a trail that Liverpool would never regret.

LIVERPOOL IN THE FOOTBALL LEAGUE

On 2 September 1893 Liverpool made their debut in the Second Division of the country's top league. Their 2-0 away victory against Middlesbrough Ironopolis — with Malcolm McVean scoring the club's first-ever Football League goal — set the tone for a glorious season. The team romped undefeated to the Second Division championship, then eliminated Newton Heath (later Manchester United), the bottom club in Division One, in a play-off to earn promotion to the top flight. McKenna's seeming impetuosity in taking the club into the Football League was completely vindicated. It looked as if the sky was the limit for the fledgling club as the First Division beckoned.

McKenna's successor: Tom Watson was the next secretary-manager of Liverpool FC

Church site: The funeral of John Houlding took place at the church of St Simon and St Jude, which stood on this site

But the bubble quickly burst: 1894/95 proved to be a disastrous season as the team plummeted to the foot of the table and crashed out of the top flight in bottom position. How could they possibly recover from such a damaging blow to their pride? But recover they did – and in style. Showing remarkable character and tenacity, they bounced back at the first attempt, winning the title on goal difference from Manchester City. Ever the man of vision, McKenna took this as his cue to step down as secretary-manager and find a replacement with the experience and track record to take the club to even greater heights of success. He wanted the best, and the best was Tom Watson.

Watson had already won the First Division Championship three times with Sunderland and had assembled an awesome team with the nickname 'the team of all talents'. Again McKenna's powers of persuasion came into their own as Watson agreed to leave the north-east, the scene of his magnificent triumphs, and head for the uncertainty of a new challenge on Merseyside.

Watson set about building his new Liverpool team slowly and carefully, laying foundations to ensure long-term success. He made a promising start, the club finishing fifth in his first season, although it was followed the next year by a dip to ninth. This didn't matter, as the following season, 1898/99, Watson's team proved good enough to chase the mighty Aston Villa – three times league champions and three times FA Cup winners – all the way in a thrilling race towards the title. In the end it was Villa who snatched it by the narrow margin of only two points, but it looked as if Liverpool would soon be after their laurels.

Classy Villa, with their squad of top-quality players, took their fifth league title the following season, but this time there was no threat from Liverpool who finished a disappointing 10th. However, showing remarkable resilience, Watson's team quickly put their disappointment behind them and with great tenacity and determination battled their way through the 1900/01 season to land the biggest prize of all – the Football League championship. McKenna's faith in Watson had been fully justified. Liverpool, the club that John Houlding had formed only nine years previously, now sat at the very pinnacle of English football. Ironically, the team they had pipped to the title was Watson's former club, Sunderland.

THE DEATH OF HOULDING AND RECONCILIATION WITH EVERTON
Houlding must have been overjoyed to see how far his club had come in such a short time. The split had been a traumatic time for everyone, and no one could possibly have predicted what kind of future lay ahead for Everton and Liverpool once they had gone their separate ways. It was certainly beyond anyone's wildest imagination that Liverpool should rise to prominence in such an incredibly short space of time.

Five years later, in 1906, Watson's Liverpool team again took the league championship, making it a magnificent Merseyside double as Everton won the FA Cup for the first time. But, sadly, Houlding, the man who had done so much to lay the foundations of Everton's and Liverpool's success, did not live long enough to see the simultaneous flowering of the two clubs he had inspired as president. He had died four years earlier at the age of 69.

Houlding had been in poor health for some time and had taken no active part in the management of Liverpool, although he did keep in regular

Cup-winners: The 1906 Everton team with the FA Cup – the first time they won the trophy

contact with the officials and players. It was hoped that his health might benefit from a trip to the warm climate of the French Riviera, but it turned out to be a false hope. He died at 7.15am on Monday 17 March 1902 at the Hotel-Pension Thomson in Cimiez near Nice. When the news broke in Liverpool, there was deep shock. Curtains were drawn in many homes and the flags at Anfield – and, significantly, at Goodison Park – were flown at half-mast. His body was brought back from France to rest at home in Stanley House prior to the funeral at the church of St Simon and St Jude just a short distance down the road.

It was Houlding's death that proved to be the decisive turning point in the relationship between Everton and Liverpool. It was exactly 10 years since the split, but during this time Everton had come to realise they owed as much to Houlding as Liverpool did. He had found grounds for Everton when they would otherwise have been homeless; he had created a solid infrastructure for the club, often injecting cash from his own pocket when it was most needed; he had recruited a management team that won the Football League championship in 1891. As Keates says in his 1928 history of Everton:

> 'The breach caused great bitterness of feeling, which, after a time, gradually subsided. For many years the directors and members of Liverpool and Everton have been on friendly terms.'

Not surprisingly, in view of Houlding's standing as a former Lord Mayor, past president of the city's two great football clubs, prominent Freemason, and highly respected charity worker, his funeral on Friday 21 March was a grand affair with representatives of many organisations in attendance. One

of those organisations was Everton Football Club. The flags at Goodison Park were already flying at half-mast but the presence of Dr James Clement Baxter as one of Everton's representatives, the man who had secured Goodison Park as the club's new base, was an even more significant gesture.

But without doubt there was no act of forgiveness and reconciliation more symbolic than the choice of the pallbearers – three Everton and three Liverpool players. They carried Houlding's coffin into the Church of St Simon and St Jude, and afterwards to his graveside in Everton Cemetery. This would have been inconceivable a few years earlier, and it gave a massive impetus to the process of healing that had already begun.

The reconciliation between Everton and Liverpool would undoubtedly have warmed the heart of the Reverend Ben Chambers who had set the ball rolling that led to the birth of both clubs. In the course of his second spell at St Domingo's from 1890-94 he had witnessed, practically at first hand, the devastating effects of the split. As the painful events at Anfield began to unfold, he could not possibly have failed to notice the immense strain his organist George Mahon, one of the key personnel in the struggle, was under.

Chambers would have felt great joy and huge relief at the positive outcome of Houlding's funeral but, sadly, he had himself died only a few months previously on 28 October 1901 at the age of 56. However, his story is far from over. In 2008, more than 100 years after his death, his grave was to be the focus of another amazing expression of unity between the two clubs, as we shall discover in the final chapter of this book.

CHAPTER 8
RECONCILIATION CONTINUES – THE MCKENNA-CUFF FRIENDSHIP

Friends first: Despite working for different clubs, WC Cuff, the Everton chairman (left), and John McKenna (above), shared a very close friendship

MCKENNA'S ACHIEVEMENTS

The expression of unity at Houlding's funeral in 1902 was a hugely significant breakthrough in restoring the relationship between Everton and Liverpool after the acrimonious split of 1892. But there was to be another remarkable gesture of friendship between the clubs about 30 years later when Liverpool FC's renowned trailblazer John McKenna died.

McKenna, it will be remembered, was the man who took Liverpool into the Football League and led them to the First Division. After handing over the reins of the team to Watson in 1896, McKenna concentrated on administration. This was not a backwards step. In the course of the next 40 years up to his death he carved a name for himself as a brilliant administrator, not only at Liverpool but also on the national stage as the highly respected and longest-serving president of the Football League.

He served Liverpool FC faithfully for 30 years. He was vice-chairman from 1900-09; chairman from 1909-1914, and again from 1917-19; and remained a director until 1922. During his years with the club, he saw Liverpool win the Football League championship three times and reach the FA Cup final. It was McKenna who in 1906 developed the Walton Breck Road End at Anfield and transformed it into the legendary Kop.

McKenna retired from Liverpool FC in 1922 to devote his energies to the Football League, but he never lost his love for the club. He was a regular spectator at home matches and appropriately it was he who in 1928 officially opened the newly roofed and extended Kop in his capacity as president of the Football League.

McKenna was elected to the management committee of the Football League in 1902, became vice-president in 1908, and president two years later. His presidency from 1910 until his death in 1936 was the longest in the League's history. To mark this incredible achievement he was presented with a commemorative scroll and casket which are now proudly exhibited in the Liverpool FC museum. He served the League with great distinction, winning enormous admiration and respect for his integrity as a man whose word was his bond. He became known in football circles as 'Honest John'.

In addition to his service to Liverpool FC and to the Football League, McKenna was also a vice-president of the Football Association. Although an official holding the highest office, he was always available to players if they needed help or advice, and despite his awesome presence, he was very approachable and players felt perfectly free to go to him with their problems or grievances. He also took a keen interest in junior and schools football, and became actively involved with the Liverpool and District association.

FRIENDSHIP WITH WILL CUFF, LEGENDARY EVERTON CHAIRMAN

It may seem surprising, in view of McKenna's allegiance to John Houlding during the split, that he was a highly regarded figure at Everton. The Everton directors had great affection and respect for him, even to the extent of recording in their minutes of 30 April 1935 that they had 'decided to make a presentation of 100 cigars to Mr John McKenna on attaining his 81st birthday'. This warm relationship stretched back many years and was the result of McKenna's very close friendship with Will Cuff.

At one stage nothing could have seemed less likely than a friendship forming between two men who were on totally opposite sides during the split. Will Cuff, who became a member of Everton in 1891 at the age of 23, was a staunch supporter of George Mahon and welcomed the break from Anfield and John Houlding. He was one of many who bought shares in Everton to help secure Goodison Park as the club's new home. His commitment to Everton was total and he was to become one of its most loyal servants during his long life. Just as McKenna moved increasingly to the centre stage at Liverpool, so, too, did Cuff at Everton. He became a director in 1895, was secretary from 1901 to 1919, and chairman from 1921 to 1938. Like McKenna, he also became president of the Football League. Cuff was a legendary figure at Everton in the same way that McKenna was at Liverpool, and it is worth knowing more about him.

WILL CUFF AND ST DOMINGO'S

William Charles Cuff was born on 19 August 1868 at 51 Byrom Street, Liverpool. He was the son of Henry Cuff, a pork butcher and trustee of St Domingo Chapel in the Everton district of Liverpool. Will's mother, Mary, was a Welsh-speaker from Pwllheli, and there was a strong Welsh influence in the household, particularly after Mary's widowed mother came to live in the family home in Liverpool. Will was the second of eight children – four boys and four girls – born to Henry and Mary. He was educated at Liverpool College and then trained as a solicitor, eventually becoming senior partner in the firm of Cuff, Roberts and Co of Castle Street, Liverpool. Like his father, Will was to become a trustee of St Domingo's and one of the chapel's loyal servants.

The Cuff connection with St Domingo Chapel was an important one and was to have great significance in the history of Everton FC. Will's father, Henry, was one of St Domingo's first trustees. He was a Londoner who moved to Liverpool as a young man to start up a business as a pork butcher. The business thrived and Henry was eventually sufficiently well off to employ two servants when the family moved to 34 Spellow Lane in the 1870s, just round the corner from Goodison Park. One of the servants, Elizabeth Roberts, was from Amlwch in Anglesey, and no doubt Henry's wife, Mary, would have spoken to her in Welsh.

Henry was a devoted and loyal servant of the chapel. Apart from his

Golden age: League championship medal from 1915, which Everton won while Cuff was secretary

responsibilities as a trustee, he was treasurer, he sat on many different committees and he was actively involved in outreach to the local community. In addition, his home became known for the warm hospitality he and Mary extended to chapel visitors. Henry was a man of considerable authority and was called upon to discipline members or employees of the chapel whose behaviour was out of line. Despite his importance, he was a very humble man who was quite prepared to do any job asked of him. He regularly set up and shifted tables in the tea-room. After the death of his wife, he moved the considerable distance to Llay, near Wrexham, to live with his daughter and her family. Despite the distance, he never relaxed his efforts on behalf of the chapel, continuing to serve it with loyalty and devotion until his death in 1911 at the age of 75.

Will Cuff followed in his father's footsteps, becoming a loyal servant of St Domingo's. As a boy he was a member of the choir, and in 1891, at the age of just 23, he was appointed choirmaster. Three years later, on 27 June 1894, he married Jessie Ford at the chapel. Their children, Henry and Hilda, were both baptised there.

Winners again: Dixie Dean – whom Cuff brought to Everton – receives the FA Cup from the Duchess of York (later the Queen Mother) in 1933

After seven years as choirmaster, Cuff stood down. His resignation in 1898 was probably due to demands on his time as a busy solicitor and as a director of Everton. Nevertheless, he continued to serve the chapel in other ways. In May 1899 he joined his father as a trustee, and four years later he was invited to become treasurer. He was also the chapel's solicitor. Despite his resignation as choirmaster, his opinion in music matters still carried considerable sway. In 1903, when a new organist was needed, Cuff was on the selection panel with George Mahon.

It says a lot for Cuff's football abilities that when St Domingo FC was formed at the chapel, he was allowed to join in the practice matches even though he was only 10 years old. Of course, when St Domingo's became Everton FC a year later and the game was taken more seriously, there could be no place for such a youngster in the side. Cuff later joined Mount FC and Walton Breck FC but injury brought his playing days to an end.

CUFF LEADS EVERTON TO GLORY

Although Cuff was never a player with Everton, he became the most successful administrator in the club's history. He was a born leader with great vision, energy and determination. His first tastes of success were as club secretary, first in 1906 when Everton brought home the FA Cup, then in 1914/15 when the Football League championship was won. As Everton secretary, Cuff made a name for himself as an innovator, becoming the first person to take a professional club to South America for exhibition matches in 1909, and two years later creating the Central League for the reserve teams of professional clubs. He had personally managed the Everton reserve side, which rarely lost a match in his charge.

Cup kings: Dixie Dean holds the FA Cup aloft alongside his teammates before they travelled back from Wembley to Liverpool

But without doubt Will Cuff will always be remembered for his outstanding achievements as Everton chairman, a position he held from 1921 to 1938. His first major triumph was capturing the signature in 1925 of a player who was to become a legend in football history – the great Dixie Dean. Dean set the football world alight with his incredible tally of goals. When Everton won the Football League championship in 1927/28, Dean scored 60 goals, a record that has never been broken. In all games that season his amazing total was exactly 100 goals.

Dean's 44 goals in the 1931/32 campaign brought the Football League championship to Goodison Park for the second time during Cuff's chairmanship, and this was quickly followed by a glorious FA Cup run in 1933 when Everton, captained by Dean, secured the trophy after a convincing 3-0 victory against Manchester City in the final. This was the first match in which players wore numbers on their shirts: Everton one to 11, Manchester City 12 to 22. It was Will Cuff's idea.

Dean was not the only exceptional player Cuff brought to Everton. He signed another football genius in October 1936 – the legendary Tommy Lawton. Tommy was only 17 at the time and playing for Burnley, but Cuff had no hesitation in signing him. Just two seasons later, in 1938/39, Lawton justified Cuff's faith in him by scoring 34 goals to help bring the league

championship to Goodison yet again.

Cuff had always insisted that only players of the highest calibre would be bought by Everton. He once told a newspaper:

> 'Throughout its history Everton has been noted for the high quality of its football. It has always been an unwritten but rigid policy of the board, handed down from one generation of directors to another, that only the classical and stylish type of player should be signed. The kick-and-rush type has never appealed to them.'

Cuff stood down as Everton chairman at the start of the 1938/39 season to take up his position as chairman of the Football League. He could look back on his time in charge of the club with huge satisfaction. Not only had he helped establish stylish league championship and cup-winning sides but he had also masterminded improvements to Goodison Park that made it the finest stadium in Britain: it was the first with two-tiered stands on all sides. Although no longer chairman of Everton, Cuff remained a director almost to the end of his life.

Despite the fame and glory which the club had gained over the years, Cuff never forgot the debt it owed to St Domingo's, the chapel that was its birthplace. There could have been no place more suitable, therefore, than St Domingo's to hold the jubilee service to commemorate Everton's 50th anniversary in 1928. And there could have been no one at the service who more symbolised the link between club and chapel than Will Cuff, chairman of Everton and former choirmaster and trustee of St Domingo's.

THE GROWING BOND BETWEEN EVERTON AND LIVERPOOL
Although Cuff and McKenna were on opposite sides of the great divide of 1892, they were kindred spirits. They were both inspirational leaders with vision, energy and determination, and they were also brilliant administrators. Under their respective chairmanships, Everton and Liverpool ascended to new heights.

Both men possessed a commanding presence and were firm in principle, but they were not cold or aloof. Players found McKenna to be approachable and understanding while Cuff was described in the *Porcupine* magazine of 17 August 1912 as a person of 'electric individuality' whose 'breezy temperament carries with it an infectious atmosphere of geniality'.

Although John Houlding's funeral proved to be the turning point in the relationship between Everton and Liverpool, it was Cuff and McKenna who triggered a long period of active cooperation between them. In 1904, only three years after Houlding's death, the two clubs launched an official joint

In League together:
As well as being
good friends,
McKenna (left) and
Cuff both held the
office of president of
the Football League

16-page match programme, the first issue appearing on 1 September at the start of the new football season.

In the course of the next 30 years, more than 1,100 issues were produced, the format remaining largely unchanged. Team line-ups were printed according to which club was at home. For example, if Everton were at home one week, the line-ups for their first team and Liverpool's reserves were printed. The following week it would be Liverpool's first team and Everton's reserves.

The growing bond between the clubs was further in evidence in the 1904/05 season when Liverpool were involved in a three-horse race with Bolton and Manchester United for the Second Division title. In a key match at Bolton, the result of which would have a considerable bearing on Liverpool's fortunes, the Everton and Liverpool players travelled together to watch the game. Everton were in the First Division that season and were keen for Liverpool to win promotion and join them in the top flight.

There was yet another gesture of friendship two years later in 1906 when Everton won the FA Cup for the first time by defeating Newcastle United 1-0 in the final at Crystal Palace. Ironically, Everton had knocked Liverpool out of the competition 2-0 in the semi-final, yet when Cuff and the victorious Everton team arrived back in Liverpool with the trophy,

McKenna and the Liverpool directors were at Central Station to greet and congratulate them.

It is also significant that, when Everton held their jubilee dinner at the Philharmonic Hall on Wednesday 24 April 1929 to celebrate their 50th anniversary, Tom Crompton, chairman of Liverpool, was among the 600 guests. Will Cuff, who presided at the event, made the following revealing remark about him: "One other name remains that has not yet been mentioned and it is one that we directors of the Everton Football Club are delighted to mention – that of the genial chairman of our friends across the Park – Mr Tom Crompton."

In his address to the audience, Crompton explained that he was attending "in the dual capacity of representing the Liverpool Football Club and also as an old player of the Everton team". He then looked back on his days as an Everton player and expressed delight at the presence of so many other former players at the gathering. He concluded by wishing the club "good luck".

THE DEATH OF MCKENNA
In addition to their remarkable achievements with Everton and Liverpool, Cuff and McKenna became highly respected presidents of the Football League. They were also vice-presidents of the Football Association and

John McKenna's grave:
The clubs joined together
to mourn his passing

members of the International Selection Committee that picked the England team. In the course of their many football duties they travelled countless miles together, enjoying the opportunity to exchange ideas and views. There would have been much to talk about as they cared passionately about the game and met many challenges to keep it free from corruption. It was a sad irony that McKenna's concern for the game proved to be the death of him – literally.

McKenna was always fiercely opposed to any kind of gambling in football and did whatever he could to suppress it. He knew that betting on the results of matches had more than once led to match-fixing, and he found this violation of the spirit of the game repugnant. Football gambling had started in 1923 when John Moores and two friends, Colin Askham and Bill Hughes, established the Littlewood Football Pool. This was followed in 1929 by Vernon's Pools. By 1936 pools had become such big business that the Football League feared the game was in danger of losing its respectability. Furthermore, there was great concern that working men were squandering their limited income in the fruitless pursuit of instant wealth. The League decided enough was enough, and on Saturday 29 February 1936 began the famous 'Pools War' in which McKenna, as president of the Football League, took a leading part.

The League's strategy was to withhold the fixture list until 24 hours before matches were due to be played, thus making it impossible for pools companies to send out coupons in time. Even the clubs themselves had no idea who their opponents would be. But the tactic failed. The pools companies got round the problem by leaving the names of the opposing teams blank and inviting punters to guess the outcome anyway. After only two weeks the League decided to abandon their strategy and explore other alternatives. (It was not, in fact, until 1959 that a compromise was reached when the Football League established copyright of their fixtures and were given a share of the pools companies' profits.)

After a special meeting of the Football League in Manchester early in March to discuss the pools issue, McKenna was heard to say: "I wish we hadn't anything to do with these things." He then made his way to the railway station where he slipped and fell on the platform. It resulted in an injury that was to have fatal consequences.

A week later he travelled to Inverness to watch Scotland play England in an amateur international match but on the return journey he became critically ill and on arrival in Liverpool was rushed to Walton Hospital. He died in the early hours of 22 March 1936. He was 81.

EVERTON AND LIVERPOOL UNITE AT MCKENNA'S FUNERAL
The Everton directors quickly decided they wanted to show their solidarity with Liverpool at McKenna's passing. The day after his death they held a

meeting, at which the following was recorded:

> *'Secy [Secretary] reported the arrangements made for the Directors wishing to attend the funeral of the late President of the Football League. It was agreed that letters of regret be sent to the Football League & to the L'pool Football Club, the organization to which Mr McKenna had been most closely associated.'*

McKenna's funeral took place on 26 March at St Margaret's Church, Anfield. His wife had died some 20 years previously and he left no family, but there was no shortage of mourners. Enormous crowds gathered at St Margaret's and there was such a heavy volume of traffic that extra police had to be drafted in.

The funeral cortege must have been an impressive sight as it arrived at St Margaret's. The leading carriages were piled high with floral tributes, some in the form of footballs and goalposts. Every club in the Football League had sent a wreath and there were also floral tributes from the football associations of England, Ireland, Scotland, Wales, France and Germany. The tribute on a German wreath read: 'With deepest memories of a man we have always loved and respected.'

The coffin was carried into the church to the accompaniment of Chopin's funeral march, and it was followed down the aisle by three Everton and three Liverpool players. It was an expression of unity to show the clubs' mutual regard for McKenna. Representing Everton were Warney Cresswell, Charlie Gee and Ben Williams; representing Liverpool were Ernie Blenkinsop, Tommy Cooper and Fred Howe.

The 11 Liverpool directors in attendance were led by chairman WJ Harrop and vice-chairman JH Troop, while the seven Everton directors were headed by Will Cuff (chairman) and Ernest Green (vice-chairman). Dr Cecil Baxter, son of Dr James Baxter and now a director himself, was among the Everton contingent. The burial followed at Smithdown Road Cemetery, where once again a large crowd had gathered. On the route from the church to the cemetery the blinds at every house and shop had been drawn as a mark of respect.

There were many glowing tributes to McKenna from the world of football, a reflection of the high regard in which he had been held. Charles Sutcliffe, senior vice-president (later president) of the Football League, praised him in the following terms: "Honest at all times, he won universal respect... the whole world of football mourns his loss... He was a man of iron will, but of such sound judgment that he was sure of his ground." Fred Rinder, vice-president of the Football League, decribed him as "always bluff, honest and straightforward. He always kept the good of the game in view, and was

always very sympathetic towards the players, particularly when they suffered injuries. He was a wonderful man, and his death will bring a great loss to the game." But the greatest tribute of all came from his close friend, Everton chairman Will Cuff:

> *"I feel I have lost a lifelong friend. We travelled together on football business many times, and I am not looking forward to taking these journeys alone. Mr McKenna was a staunch friend, who, beneath his brusque exterior, had a heart of gold. From the Football League and Football Association point of view I think the greatest man in football has gone. He will live long in the memory of all who had anything to do with the governing of football. Fearless, outspoken, and absolutely honest, he was well named 'Honest John'. The football world in general is under a very deep sorrow."*

Cuff and one of the Liverpool directors, RL Martindale, were appointed executors of his will. McKenna did not forget his good friend Cuff, and left him his gold cufflinks and the fountain pen he had been presented by the directors of Leicester City Football Club.

CUFF UNVEILS A MEMORIAL TO MCKENNA AT ANFIELD

About a year later, at the end of February 1937, a plaque in memory of McKenna was unveiled at Anfield. There were several dignitaries from the world of football present at the ceremony, including Charles Sutcliffe, president of the Football League; Fred Howarth, secretary of the Football League; Ted Robbins, secretary of the Welsh FA; representatives of the Scottish FA; WJ Harrop, chairman of Liverpool FC; and Will Cuff, chairman of Everton FC. It was Cuff who was invited to unveil the plaque in memory of his old friend.

In the course of the ceremony Cuff handed Liverpool's chairman, WJ Harrop, a silver casket containing an address presented to McKenna by all 88 clubs in the Football League in recognition of his long and distinguished service. In his speech, Cuff told the audience they were "perpetuating the memory of a great British sportsman... No place for the memorial could be more appropriate than the headquarters of Liverpool FC where Mr McKenna was so active... He was a football genius and meritoriously earned all the honours the game had to give."

Not shying away from the past, Cuff also told the story of how McKenna had "refused to join the secessionists who trekked to Goodison Road, but took a prominent part in the foundation of the Liverpool club of which he later became chairman". Forty-five years later at the unveiling ceremony at Anfield it was obvious the split had left no lingering trace of ill feeling between the clubs. The McKenna-Cuff friendship had long since put a stop to that.

CHAPTER 9
JOINT MATCH PROGRAMMES AND FOOTBALL SUNDAYS

The reconciliation between Everton and Liverpool at John Houlding's funeral in 1902 was followed by a long and productive period of cooperation between the two clubs. It was due in no small measure to Will Cuff of Everton and John McKenna of Liverpool who, despite being on opposite sides during the split, became firm friends and worked closely together for the benefit of both clubs.

Cuff had become a director of Everton in 1895 and was appointed secretary six years later in 1901. McKenna was secretary of Liverpool at that time, having stood down as team manager to concentrate on administration. Their roles as respective club secretaries brought them into contact with each other and they soon discovered they were kindred spirits. Their influence was considerable and they created a climate of harmony and goodwill between the directors of Everton and Liverpool.

We have already seen how the two clubs joined forces in August 1903 and formed a deputation to the tramways manager insisting that the inadequate tram services to Anfield and Goodison be improved to cope with the ever-growing crowds. And we have also seen how the Liverpool directors were at Central Station to welcome and congratulate the victorious Everton team who were returning from London with the FA Cup – despite Liverpool's elimination from the competition at the hands of Everton in the semi-final.

These were key indicators of the growing friendship between the clubs, but their unity was firmly sealed when they combined to produce joint match programmes for 31 years from 1904 until 1935. Shared worship at St Domingo Chapel during the 1930s at the annual football service known as 'Football Sundays' was yet another indication of the depth of their friendship.

JOINT MATCH PROGRAMMES 1904-1935
The cooperation between the two clubs in the production of joint match programmes was never going to be a flash in the pan. There was a deep commitment to this project right from the start and it was almost certainly spearheaded by John McKenna, Liverpool's vice-chairman, and Will Cuff, secretary of Everton. They would have enjoyed the support of the new Everton chairman, Dr James Clement Baxter, who had represented Everton at John Houlding's funeral and been a member of the Everton-Liverpool deputation to the tramways department.

Incredibly, more than 1,100 programmes, each of 16 pages, were published from 1904 to 1935. But these were just the winter issues covering football. There were also summer editions reporting on a range of popular sports on Merseyside including athletics, cricket, cycling and swimming, but even baseball, bowls and quoits were catered for.

Colour-coded: Red and blue were introduced to the front of the programmes to show which club was featured – these are the first examples of each

(Images reproduced with permission from The Everton Collection Charitable Trust)

The cover design of the programme changed from time to time but the names of the two clubs were always prominently displayed, accompanied by the words 'Only Programme issued by Authority of the Everton and Liverpool Clubs'. From 1907 the word 'issued' was changed to 'published'.

At the start of the 1933/34 season, colour featured for the first time. It reflected the club playing at home. If Everton were the home team, the player depicted in the cartoon on the front cover was kitted out in a blue shirt, white shorts and blue socks and kicking a blue ball; if Liverpool, then the player was kitted out in a red shirt, white shorts and red socks and kicking a red ball.

The following season, 1934/35, the last in which the programme appeared, the cartoon was altered slightly, but again the player wore either blue or red depending on which team was at home. But now, instead of the ball changing colour, the word 'OFFICIAL' preceding 'FOOTBALL PROGRAMME' switched between blue and red.

The programme at no time showed any bias towards Everton or Liverpool. The emphasis was always on 'our' clubs. This can be seen from various reports in the programme, starting with the issue of Saturday 24 December 1904, the year collaboration began (the emphasis is mine):

> 'During the past four months we have endeavoured to make our "Programme" sufficiently attractive to appeal to the football public of this great city, and it has been a source of extreme gratification to find that our efforts have been so keenly appreciated. In our desire to further the interests of <u>our two premier clubs</u>... we have been actuated by one impulse only, to state without fear or favour what we consider would be beneficial to them.'

And the following Saturday we read:

> 'Our earnest wish is that <u>both our clubs</u> will experience "A Happy and Prosperous New Year".'

This spirit lasted throughout the 31 years. At the other end of the time scale, in the programme of Saturday 25 August 1934, the language remains much the same as in 1904. The editor writes:

> 'Of one thing we may rest assured: <u>both our</u> Everton and Liverpool players are eager and enthusiastically willing to give of their best, and should that ultimately be found not quite good enough it is equally certain that <u>our directorates</u> will not hesitate to set about strengthening any possible weak links.'

There was even a section that appeared from time to time with the sub-heading 'Our Two League Clubs' or sometimes just 'Our Two Clubs' with a summary of the fortunes of both teams.

The programmes offer a remarkable source of information at many levels. In fact, one of the very early contributors said that to call the publication a programme was 'rather a misnomer as it is in reality a little paper'. He makes a good point. These 'little papers' give us much more than team line-ups, results and league tables. They are also a mine of information about personalities at the clubs and important developments that have shaped their history. They also give an insight into football history generally and allow fascinating glimpses into social history, showing us the fashions people wore, the entertainment they enjoyed and the drinks they drank.

Under appropriate sub-headings, this chapter will highlight articles that shed light on some of the more important events in Everton's and Liverpool's history. To give the reader a flavour of the attitudes and language of the time, the original wording will be used wherever possible.

THE PROGRAMME INTRODUCES ITSELF

The very first issue appeared on Thursday 1 September 1904. It was for Liverpool's home match – a 5.30 evening kick-off – against Burton United. The editor took the opportunity to introduce the programme and explain its purposes:

> 'THE NEW PROGRAMME: Today we make our bow to the Liverpool public for the first time. We trust that our effort will please the football crowd... We are all enthusiasts, following the game for the sake of sport, and it is our intention to do all for the best interests and traditions of the game. Every endeavour will be made to obtain the correct teams, and we have been assured of assistance from all quarters. The Directors of Everton and Liverpool, and the respective Secretaries, Mr WC Cuff and Mr Tom Watson, and all the officials, have already given us every consideration, and we thank them sincerely.'

Apart from informing its readers about football matters, the programme also offered a weekly guide to the shows and plays at Liverpool's theatres. It was called 'Before the Footlights' and commanded a double-page spread. The first article in the series adopts a somewhat cautious tone:

> 'In taking up a new column one often wonders who and what the readers are... A visit to the arena at Goodison Park and Anfield Road puts a writer at once in touch with his audience. He sees it before him, and it is for him to judge what matter will suit that audience best. It is a difficult question to please everybody, but the football crowd is

Where it started: Front cover (right) and inside the first Everton/Liverpool joint matchday programme. It was produced for Liverpool's home game against Burton United on Thursday 1 Sept 1904. Images (c) The Everton Collection Charitable Trust

so cosmopolitan that in dealing with the various shows in and around Liverpool it is just possible to say something that will appeal to everybody.'

'EVERTON JOTTINGS' AND 'ANFIELD HAPPENINGS'

During the 31 years of the programme's production, two sections regularly appeared under the headings of 'Everton Jottings' and 'Anfield Happenings'. They reported on team progress and developments at the respective clubs.

The first issue of 1 September 1904 looks ahead to the new season and considers the prospects of the two clubs. (On this occasion, 'Anfield Happenings' went under the heading of 'Liverpool Longings'.) The rather quaint language strikes us as amusing today and it is hard to imagine that these pieces were written with cloth-capped working men on the terraces in mind.

'EVERTON JOTTINGS: The dawn of another season is at hand, with its wealth of budding hopes for the future, and everywhere are noticeable signs of reviving life in the football world, after a four months' period of slumber... This preliminary period is in a sense a

pleasurable one, for we can indulge in dreams of future triumphs, undimmed by the thoughts of unexpected reverses; it is indeed the spring time of the football year.

'A year ago [Everton] had a splendid chance of winning the League Championship, but an unaccountable trio of blunders in three home games destroyed the opportunity... However, let those failings of the team be swept into the oblivion of the past... There is every reason to feel confident about the coming campaign.'

'LIVERPOOL LONGINGS: The longings of Liverpool are known to all. They are to get back into the first division as quickly as possible. For the third time Liverpool have to fight their way upwards, and what they accomplished aforetime, they ought to have no difficulty in doing again. The fall of the Livers is now an old story. Through the defection of certain players they were a different team to the one that won the Championship, and right throughout the season they were under a cloud.

'What are Liverpool's chances of again being first Leaguers? Well, I

believe they have a team able to win the League Championship let alone the second.'

Were the hopes expressed in these two pieces justified? In both cases, yes. Everton finished runners-up in the First Division, one position higher than the previous season, while Liverpool won the Second Division championship to earn promotion.

It was interesting to note that Liverpool were referred to as 'The Livers'. This nickname probably came into use in 1901 when the club incorporated the Liver Bird into its crest. It was used for many years before 'The Reds' became the accepted nickname.

THE HOULDING FAMILY'S BREAK WITH LIVERPOOL

A bombshell was dropped at Liverpool's Annual Meeting in October 1904 when it was announced that William Houlding, John Houlding's son and the owner of the club, had decided to sever his connection with Anfield. The programme of Saturday 29 October 1904 contained the following account:

'CHANGES AT ANFIELD: The announcement that Mr William Houlding has decided to sever his connection with the Liverpool club came upon us with mixed feelings. We have been so accustomed to look upon the two as being indissolubly associated that the separation caused us to experience a regretful pang. But on further consideration we are convinced that ultimate benefit will ensue from the change, a statement which we make without any desire to depreciate the invaluable services which the Houlding family have at various times rendered to the Anfield organisations.

'Under a more popular form of control, the club should make even greater headway in the future than it has done in the past, and, from a purely football point of view, we should imagine it will be advantageous to possess free and unrestricted powers in the management thereof.

'Mr Houlding's departure is deeply regrettable, but the generous manner in which he has met the suggested new company constitutes a fitting termination to a long and honourable connection.'

William Houlding's departure signalled a change at the top. Edwin Berry, the new Anfield supremo, was a Liverpool solicitor with a strong background in football as a player – with Everton! The same programme gives the details:

Where it ended: After 31 years of working together, the clubs' last-ever joint programme for a league match came out in May 1935 (above) although a souvenir edition followed. Image (c) The Everton Collection Charitable Trust

'New Chairman Mr Edwin Berry was born in Liverpool, in the Everton district, and as a youth helped to form the Saint Domingo Club, practically the first football club in Liverpool, and out of which the Everton Football Club sprang... During his connection with Everton the Liverpool Cup was first put up for competition, and he was a member of the Everton team which won it in its first year... Edwin Berry played with Everton for several seasons.'

The final break with the Houlding family was confirmed a few months later in the programme of Saturday 25 February 1905 in which it was announced that

'...the Houlding family would surrender the 2,000 shares they held, and would forego their claims for £10,000 spent by the late Alderman Houlding in founding the club if they were relieved of the guarantee which the bank holds for £5,000.'

THE SPIRIT OF THE LOCAL DERBIES
Much has been said of the goodwill that had been developing between the clubs, but what of the derby matches? What happened when Blue met Red? Did the old feelings of animosity engendered by the split surface in these confrontations?

Two reports from the early years of the programme give us an answer. On Saturday 30 September 1905 we read:

'BLUE VERSUS RED: One of the greatest local fights of the year occurs this afternoon at Goodison Park. That partisanship will run high is indisputable, and, truth to tell, we should not care to see it otherwise. We are confidently anticipating a well-fought struggle, and thanks to the good common sense of the respective players of the two clubs, who have long since recognised the fact that they are there to play football and not to engender sectarian bitterness, there are substantial grounds for such expectations being realised.'

A year later, Saturday 22 September 1906, the picture was much the same:

'RED VERSUS BLUE: Next week we should see a battle royal at Anfield, when the League Champions [Liverpool] will measure swords with the holders of the English Cup [Everton]... The days are happily gone when such an anticipation as this was utterly out of the question, and in recent years our men have shown how to control their personal feelings. We can thus view the keenest of rivals at play, and still be charmed by the excellence of their football.'

EVERTON, LIVERPOOL AND NEEDY CAUSES
Everton and Liverpool have always been involved in schemes to improve the lives of the poor and needy. The reports below are of two of their early charity initiatives.

Thursday 1 September 1904:

'FOOTBALL AND CHARITY: The suggestion that a nominal charge of a penny should be made for admission to the practice matches of the various League clubs in the country has been taken up with practical unanimity by all our leading organizations. As a result, various deserving institutions, to whom the proceeds have to be devoted, have benefited considerably, and our two premier clubs have reason to feel gratified with the response which has been made by the public at their preliminary trials.

'About £115 was taken at the Liverpool club's headquarters, and the whole of this has been handed over to the Hospital Saturday Fund. Equally gratifying were the takings at Goodison Park, the amount being close on £125, and this will be apportioned to the Stanley Hospital and Hospital Saturday Fund. Footballers are never found wanting when the claims of charity are brought to their notice.'

Saturday 14 October 1905:

'THE UNEMPLOYED: Mr Cuff [Everton secretary] has forwarded a proposal to the Lord Mayor which should meet with the approval of all. The fight for the Liverpool Cup will take place at Goodison Park on a date to be arranged, and it is suggested that the net proceeds should be divided into three parts, Liverpool to take one, Everton one, and one to go to the unemployed fund. Needless to say, Liverpool cordially agree with the proposal.'

THE PIONEERS OF GOODISON PARK
The events leading up to the split of 1892 and Everton's migration to Goodison Park have been well documented. However, the article below from the programme of Saturday 14 March 1914 gives a fresh understanding of the enormous effort needed to get Goodison Park ready in time for the start of the 1892/93 season. The article was prompted by an award to Everton director John Davies for his 21 years' service to the club.

'Having served the Everton club faithfully and well for twenty-one years, Mr John Davies, Director, is to receive some slight appreciation of his services therein. Of the stalwarts who, in the year 1892, laid the

foundations of Everton's greatness the younger generation know but little. They, however, have the privilege of enjoying the results which these pioneers of the club, by their energy, determination, and unstinted labours made possible. In April of that year, the seceders... made arrangements for securing the present plot of ground in Goodison Road, and Mr Davies was one of the signatories of the lease drawn up for its acquisition.

'There was ample work for every director in those days, real spade work, and these pioneers never spared themselves; they gave their time, money, and energies, willingly... They had two months in which to get everything ready – July to September – the laying out of the playing pitch, the stands, offices, and various other matters incidental to the equipment of a football club's enclosure. Every spare minute between business hours was given up to the work in hand, from early morn to dewey eve, not a moment was wasted, but everything was done willingly and enthusiastically to ensure the success which subsequently followed... Those pioneers, amongst whom [John Davies] was most prominent, are deserving of our highest esteem and regard.'

EVERTON AND LIVERPOOL IN THE FIRST WORLD WAR

When the First World War broke out in September 1914, the Football Association and the Football League were faced with a very tough decision. The Rugby Football Union had almost immediately suspended all rugby activities; should football do likewise? In the face of accusations of unpatriotic behaviour, even cowardice, football's decision-makers took the opposite path and opted to keep the league programme and FA Cup competition running.

The decision was followed by howls of protests and a heated campaign to try and shut football down. Feelings ran so high that some grammar schools switched to rugby union in protest. The following letter to the *Liverpool Daily Post* on 27 March 1917 about the large crowd at the Everton-Liverpool derby match voices the concern of many: 'At Goodison Park on Saturday, a crowd of 25,000 people watched a game of football between the Everton and Liverpool clubs. A very considerable percentage of that assembly must have been of fighting age.'

The debate raged throughout the years of the First World War, and the extracts below from various joint Everton-Liverpool match programmes give some indication of the bitter criticism the two clubs had to face. We also learn something about the intense pressures the players were under.

Saturday 26 September 1914:

'Those pessimists who would have us go about with long-drawn faces and mournful looks, who would dispense with every form of amusement, especially football, during this war time are being effectually thrust aside. Healthy recreation is a wholesome tonic that will tend to counteract the sorrow and misery caused by this terrible war, and will not make the people of this country one whit less able or willing to fight the foe.

'The attendance at Anfield last Saturday showed conclusively that there are thousands of people... who need the customary League match, which is their only outdoor enjoyment during the winter months.'

Saturday 12 December 1914:

'By a large majority the Football Association have decided that their Cup Competition shall continue this season. No doubt this determination on the part of the FA will lead to another outpouring from the agitators, accompanied by an avalanche of more sentimental slobbering.

'What substantial reason can be advocated for stopping football because the nation is at war? It is the cultivation of the sporting spirit which has been inculcated into the characters of Englishmen that has stimulated our soldiers to the deeds of valour which they have performed in this war. When Sir Francis Drake was informed of the approach of the Spanish Armada, he refused to stop the game of bowls which he was then playing.

'The panic-mongers would have us believe that by continuing football we are a menace to the country, and are lacking in patriotism. It is absurd to imagine that by stopping the sport the destinies of the war would be influenced in the slightest degree.'

Saturday 20 November 1915:

'Our two clubs are being well patronised by the football-loving public of this city and the surrounding districts, which simply goes to prove that the authorities acted wisely when they determined to continue the game during the war time.

'Deprived of their wages at one fell swoop, our footballers have engaged themselves in munition works and other Government employment, and have also come forward and provided thousands of persons with a delightful entertainment each week either at Anfield or Goodison Park.

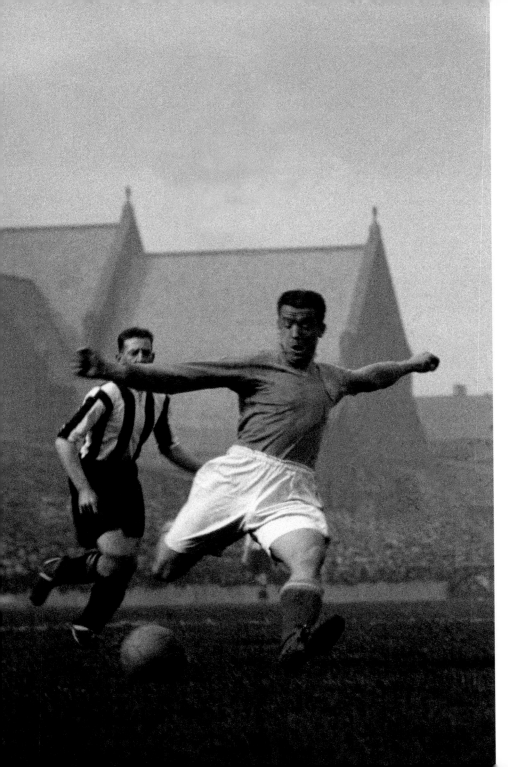

Unstoppable: While the joint programmes were being produced, Dixie Dean set a new goalscoring record of 60 goals in a season. His achievement was dealt with very briefly in the publication

'Had those superior persons who can see nothing good in the people's pastimes been allowed to have their way thousands of weary workers would have been rendered more moody and morbid by the blank Saturday afternoons.'

Saturday 27 December 1915:

'Both our clubs have nobly fulfilled their mission; they have provided the public with entertaining exhibitions of football through a depressing period and helped them to preserve a cheerful spirit.

'We feel that a great debt of gratitude is due to the players at Goodison Park and Anfield for the splendid manner in which they have responded to the calls upon them. Their wages were entirely stopped, and then they were asked to come forward and play football for the benefit of the sport-loving community. They are all engaged in work which has an important bearing on the war; some on munitions, others on engineering needs, whilst there are those who are toiling in the coal mines. When it is borne in mind that they are occupied sometimes day and night and not always under the most inviting surroundings, some allowance should be made for any lapses of form that they may show when on the football field.

'We should like to impress this fact upon the spectators who are in the habit of attending the games at Goodison Park and Anfield. If the players make mistakes they should be encouraged and not ridiculed; they are doing their best and are keeping the game alive at a time when many superior people in the country, who have always despised it because it was the sport of the masses, would like to see it wiped out.'

On a different note, the following report in the programme of Saturday 16 April 1916 tells how Everton and Liverpool did what they could to lift the spirits of injured soldiers who could sometimes number up to 4,000 at a single match.

'It is a matter of common knowledge to those who have visited our grounds at Anfield and Goodison Park this season that the number of men in khaki has been pronounced. Special entrances have been allotted to these gallant fellows; they have been admitted free, and extra privileges have been granted to these wounded heroes, who having done their duty at the front have returned maimed and handicapped, and who need some little enjoyment and recreation to make them forget the horrors of war.'

DIXIE DEAN SETS A NEW GOALS RECORD

One of the most outstanding achievements in football history is Dixie Dean's tally of 60 league goals in a single season. The fact that the Everton marksman accomplished this in the top flight of English football and set a record that has never been broken gives some indication of his amazing talent. And yet, in the final home match of the season against Arsenal on Saturday 5 May 1928, when Dean was poised to break the existing record, the match programme is remarkably low-key, giving this only a passing mention.

This surprises us today, living as we do in a celebrity culture, but it must be remembered that in Dean's time football was considered a team sport and no individual player was glorified in the way he would be now. In a reasonably lengthy article, Dean gets only two brief mentions. The key extracts are printed below:

'The Blues wound up a brilliant series of away victories by defeating Burnley at Turf Moor [5-3. Dean scored 4]... Seeing that the home team were anxious to improve their position, the triumph of our players was all the more meritorious.

'There was no suggestion of end of the season football in this game and the occasion served for Dean to bring his toll of goals to within two of Camsell's Second Division record of last season.

'After the contest today the team will make ready for their tour in Switzerland... Dean will take part in representative games against France in Paris (17th), and against Belgium in Antwerp (19th).'

When Everton met Tranmere in the final of the Liverpool Senior Cup two days later, Dean had already scored the hat-trick that set a new record. And yet the report in 'Everton Jottings' in the Monday programme was exactly the same as in the previous Saturday's, with the addition of just five words (which I have emphasised in italics): 'The occasion served for Dean to bring his toll of goals to within two of Camsell's Second Division record of last season, *which was surpassed on Saturday.*' A remarkable understatement!

THE IMPACT OF RADIO COMMENTARIES

Developments in communications technology tend to be warmly welcomed today. After all, where would we be without the internet, satellite TV or mobile phones? Yet it hasn't always been like this. An extract from the programme of Saturday 4 May 1935 sees things in a quite different light.

The previous Saturday Everton had beaten Bury 3-1 in the final of the Lancashire Cup, the same afternoon that Sheffield Wednesday had won

Football Sundays: Reverend David Rowlands Rowe, who conducted services for footballers of the two clubs between 1935 and 1939 (left). Above: His daughters Betty Yorke and Gwynneth Rowe with Peter Lupson

the FA Cup after a 4-2 victory against West Bromwich Albion. But according to the joint Everton-Liverpool, all was not well:

'After being a distinct success in all rounds leading up to the Final, Saturday's gate in the Lancashire Cup proved a decided "flop"...There is no doubt the FA Cup Final broadcast was the chief reason the crowd stayed at home.

'No wonder the poorer clubs up and down the country object to football "on the air". We have only to look at the miserable gates obtaining at nearly every League match on Saturday in proof of this.'

THE LAST JOINT PROGRAMME

After 31 years of successful collaboration on match programmes, the clubs finally decided to produce individual issues at the start of the 1935/36 season. The last-ever joint programme was, therefore, the souvenir edition published on Saturday 11 May 1935 for the match at Goodison Park between England and a combined Wales-Ireland team. The game was held in celebration of the 25th anniversary of the reign of King George V and

Queen Mary, and all proceeds were donated to the Royal Jubilee Fund. Perhaps a match of such importance was the appropriate way to mark the end of a unique era of programme production.

FOOTBALL SUNDAYS

The fact that the clubs had decided to print separate match programmes from the autumn of 1935 did not in any way suggest a rift had developed between them. In fact, quite the opposite was the case. An unmistakable sense of unity was witnessed at John McKenna's funeral in March 1936, and a further bond was also evident at the annual football services known as 'Football Sundays'. These were held at St Domingo Chapel during the 1930s and both clubs joined together there in worship.

From 1935-39 the footballers' services at St Domingo's were conducted by its minister, the Reverend David Rowlands Rowe. His daughters, Betty Yorke and Gwynneth Rowe, both now in their 90s, told me of their memories of them. They recall that the services were held in the evenings and were so popular that, even though they were the minister's daughters, they had to have an early tea to ensure they would get a seat. Fortunately, they didn't have far to go. The manse where the minister's family lived was at No 3 St Domingo Grove, almost next door to the chapel.

Interestingly, current Liverpool chief executive Rick Parry has family connections with the area. His mother grew up at No 1 St Domingo Grove next door to the manse, and she remembers the Rowe family well. Mr Parry told me that he used to kick a ball against the St Domingo wall which backed on to his grandparents' garden, and if he miskicked it he had to climb over the wall to retrieve it.

Betty and Gwynneth recall that there were long queues outside the chapel on Football Sundays, which is hardly surprising in view of the famous names who attended the services. Among the Everton contingent would be Dixie Dean and Tommy Lawton, while Matt Busby (later to become the legendary Manchester United manager) and Berry Nieuwenhuys were among the Liverpool players. The Lord Mayor of Liverpool also attended.

Inside the chapel there was no formal seating arrangement nor any kind of division based on club membership. It was a relaxed and happy occasion. Perhaps Betty's recollections of the informal manner in which the players mingled at the services provide the ideal end to this chapter:

'They didn't go in serried ranks like you see at funerals now. They went because they were neighbours and friends. They would just be dotted about in family groups in the congregation. There wasn't the rivalry between football teams in those days. It was all very friendly.'

Family connection: Rick Parry's grandparents lived at No 1 St Domingo Grove, next to the manse – the house is at the left-hand end of the building pictured opposite, nearest to the church. Parry's grandmother is pictured above, in the centre, and the wall that he used to kick a ball against is in the background

CHAPTER 10
EVERTON, LIVERPOOL AND THE MOORES ERA

There are few people who have exerted a greater influence on the fortunes of Everton and Liverpool Football Clubs than John Moores, the multi-millionaire who founded the vast Littlewoods empire. As well as his pools and chain store interests, Moores also had a consuming passion for football and invested vast sums of money in both clubs. But, just as importantly, he had the uncanny knack of finding the right people for the right job at the right time. It was Moores who brought the legendary Everton manager Harry Catterick to Goodison Park, and he also had a hand in bringing the immortal Bill Shankly to Anfield. For these reasons alone his name would go down in football folklore, but he contributed much more. In fact, the years in which he and his family shaped events at Anfield and Goodison Park have become known as 'The Moores Era'. In any history of Everton or Liverpool it is impossible to avoid the name of John Moores. His story deserves to be told.

JOHN MOORES: THE EARLY YEARS

For all his wealth and success, John Moores did not have the advantage of a privileged background. He was born the son of a bricklayer on 25 January 1896 in Eccles, Manchester, one of eight children. He left school at 14 to work as a messenger boy for the Post Office in Manchester, but even at this early age his drive and ambition were apparent. Determined to improve himself, he studied telegraphy at the Post Office School of Telegraphy in evening classes, and this led to a job two years later as a junior operator with the Commercial Cable Company. After only a year he was upgraded to operator and transferred to Bradford.

At the age of 20 he joined the Royal Navy, serving during the First World War as a wireless telegraphist. When the war was over he resumed his employment with the Commercial Cable Company and was posted to Liverpool. Shortly afterwards, in 1919, tragedy struck his family when his father died of alcoholism at the age of 47, leaving 23-year-old John Moores as the principal breadwinner. The two youngest children in the family, both sisters, were only nine and 10 years old.

Moores had the strength of character to cope with this blow and his subsequent responsibilities. In fact, he actually attributed much of his later success in life to the pressures he had to endure in his early years. He once said: "I've had an advantage over my sons in that they haven't had adversity to sharpen them a little. If life is too easy, you don't get on."

And 'get on' he certainly did. When the Cable Company transferred him to a remote station in Waterville on the south-west tip of County Kerry, Ireland, in 1921 to work on transatlantic cables, his entrepreneurial instincts found their first outlet. In his spare time he set up a shopping club called the Waterville Supplies Company, and sold books, fountain pens and stationery to employees of the Cable Company.

A new era: Statue of the founders of the Littlewoods business empire, John Moores (left) and Cecil Moores, in Old Hall Street, Liverpool. John (above) played a significant part in the growth and success of both Everton and Liverpool

Moores was able to buy these items in bulk from sources in Dublin or Britain out of the savings he had accumulated. His mother had instilled in him the importance of saving and he often spoke of the influence she had had on him: "I was taught thrift by my mother. She used to give threepence a week pocket money, and as an incentive to put it away I was promised a halfpennorth of sweets if I saved!"

THE BIRTH OF LITTLEWOODS FOOTBALL POOL
After 18 months in Waterville, the Cable Company transferred Moores back to Liverpool. It was here that his next business venture was born. Convinced that betting on the results of football matches could be a profitable business, Moores set up a new company with two friends, Colin Askham and Bill Hughes. The idea was to sell coupons with match fixtures and offer cash prizes for guessing the correct results. The prizes would be taken from the pool of money collected from the sale of coupons (hence 'football pool').

As all three were employees of the Cable Company, they were not permitted to undertake any kind of outside work. To set up in business on their own they would have to hide their identities. They soon found a solution. One of the three, Colin Askham, had been orphaned as a baby and brought up by an aunt. His real name was Colin Littlewood but he had been given the surname Askham after his aunt had assumed responsibility for him. The Cable Company would never connect the name 'Littlewood' with any of the three young entrepreneurs and so it was decided to call their enterprise 'The Littlewood Football Pool'.

At the beginning of the 1923/24 season the three partners each contributed £50 to finance the cost of printing and distributing coupons. It was a considerable sum in those days and Moores recalls his feelings as he made that payment: "As I signed my own cheque at the bank, my hands were damp. It seemed such a lot of money to be risking."

The new company began life in a small, rented office in Church Street, Liverpool. However, despite initial optimism, the venture seemed doomed to failure. Initially, 4,000 coupons had been printed and small boys hired to distribute them outside Manchester United's ground before a Saturday home match. But only 35 coupons were returned. Undeterred by this setback, Moores and his friends printed another 10,000 for distribution outside Hull City's ground. The response was even worse – only one was returned. By the end of the season all three partners had lost £600. The writing was on the wall.

Askham and Hughes decided to pull out and cut their losses but Moores was determined to carry on. He, too, had felt like throwing in the towel, but his wife, Ruby, persuaded him otherwise. She told him: "I would rather be married to a man who is haunted by failure than one haunted by regret." Moores bought his partners out, paying them £200 each to cover

their losses in return for their shares. He continued the business with the help of Ruby, his brother Cecil, and one of his sisters.

It proved to be the best business decision he ever made. By the end of the second season, the number of returned coupons reached 10,000; by the end of the third season the figure was 20,000. The company prospered and after three years Moores was in a position to give up his job with the Cable Company and devote himself entirely to his pools business. It grew at a breathtaking rate and by 1932, when he was only 36, Moores had become a millionaire.

LITTLEWOODS CHAIN STORES AND MAIL ORDER COMPANIES
With the capital he had acquired, Moores placed the pools company in his brother Cecil's hands and turned his business skills to other areas. In 1932 he founded the Littlewoods Mail Order Store, running the business from a small office in Whitechapel, Liverpool. It was a novel idea. Groups of 20 people each paid one shilling (10p) per week into a club for 20 weeks. This generated a £1 pool each week. At the end of the week a draw was held and the winner received £1 worth of household goods. The business made huge profits and within four years the annual turnover was £4 million.

Having made a success of his mail order company, Moores looked for a new challenge. He opened his first department store in Blackpool in July 1937. This did so well that others quickly followed and within two years Moores had a chain of 24 stores in different parts of the country. At its peak, the business eventually numbered more than 120 stores. In 1991 two stores were opened in St Petersburg, the first by a major Western retailer in the Soviet Union.

During the Second World War, Moores offered the services of his Littlewoods organisation to the Government. He made available 16 factories and over 14,000 people to help the war effort. Their output was phenomenal. Littlewoods became the biggest producers of parachutes in the country, making some five million, but its employees also produced 12 million shells, six million fuses, 700 fuselages for Wellington bombers, 50,000 rubber dinghies and 20,000 barrage balloons.

After the war, Moores branched out into credit mail order, selling goods selected from a catalogue and paid for in instalments. His first such company was Burlington, launched in 1952. This was followed by Brian Mills (1953), Littlewood's Warehouses (1954), Janet Frazer (1964) and Peter Craig (1968). During the 1970s the annual sales from these companies climbed from £113 million to a staggering £673 million. Incredibly, they despatched 40 million parcels a year between them.

JOHN MOORES'S WEALTH AND HONOURS
John Moores eventually became one of the richest men in the world. In 1981

the *Guinness Book of Records* estimated his fortune to be worth £1,200 million. For all his wealth, Moores did not live the high life. He didn't smoke, rarely drank, had no yachts, and his four-bedroom house in Freshfield, near Formby, was not palatial. He contributed generously to charitable causes and he was a patron of the arts, sponsoring a biennial art exhibition at the Walker Art Gallery in Liverpool to promote young painters.

He received many honours. In 1970 he was awarded Liverpool's highest honour – the freedom of the city. This was followed in 1972 by the CBE for his work for youth scholarship and handicapped children, and in 1973 by the honorary degree of Doctor of Laws of Liverpool University. In June 1980 he was knighted for his services to art. When Liverpool Polytechnic was granted university status in 1992, the institution was named Liverpool John Moores University after him. In 1996 a bronze statue to John and Cecil Moores was unveiled in Church Street, Liverpool, to mark the centenary of John Moores's birth.

What was the secret of his phenomenal success? He tells us in his own words:

"Any person who is prepared to work five or 10 per cent harder than the next man is bound to succeed. The man who wants to get on in life must be prepared to put in that bit extra. Obviously he needs intelligence, but he needs energy and enthusiasm to an even greater degree."

He also insisted:

"There should be much more than the profit motive in any business which is going to be really successful. The customer has got to be given a fair deal."

And in another interview he made it clear that a company's staff must also be given a fair deal.

JOHN MOORES AND HIS LINKS WITH EVERTON AND LIVERPOOL
In his younger days John Moores was a keen amateur footballer, playing until he was 45. He and his brother Cecil were regular members of the Littlewoods works team. He also loved to watch the game, and soon after arriving in Liverpool he became a passionate supporter of Everton. One of his abiding memories was witnessing Dixie Dean score his record-breaking 60th league goal in a season in the match against Arsenal at Goodison Park on 5 May 1928. He continued to watch Everton play until he was well into his 80s, despite failing health.

In addition to being a keen Everton supporter, he was also the club's largest shareholder. In 1960 he was elected to the board and served the club faithfully as director and chairman for 17 years. His son, John, was also a shareholder of the club.

Despite his love for Everton, Moores had great affection for Liverpool and watched them play at Anfield whenever Everton were not at home. He once commented:

"It's good for the city to have two first-class clubs. Of course, being an Evertonian I want them to be above Liverpool – but I still want them to do well."

On another occasion he remarked: "So long as we have one of the teams in the news I am quite happy."

As well as watching Liverpool play in those early years, he also bought shares in the club. He later became Liverpool's largest shareholder, but he never cashed in the dividends he was paid, preferring that the club should keep the money. But his support for the club went even further than this. When Liverpool decided to erect new stands on the Anfield Road and Kemlyn Road sides of their stadium in the 1960s, Moores provided the services of his own architects and lawyers entirely free of charge. This represented a massive saving for the club of approximately two million pounds in today's terms.

Moores's sons John and Peter also had shares in Liverpool, thus ensuring a close link between the club and the Moores family. That link was to become even closer when Moores's nephew, David, was elected Liverpool chairman in 1991, a position he was to hold for 16 years until 2007. But more about David later.

MOORES BRINGS HARRY CATTERICK TO EVERTON
Despite his obvious affection for Liverpool, John Moores's name will always be closely associated with Everton. He became actively involved with the club during the Second World War through his friendship with Dick Searle, the majority shareholder. When Searle found himself in financial difficulties, he sold half his shares to Moores. Later, when the club was unable to install floodlights because of a credit squeeze at the bank, Moores lent them the money. It was obvious that he cared about the club, and he was eventually persuaded to join the board in March 1960. On 23 June 1960 he was appointed chairman. It was the start of a great era in Everton's history.

Although the team finished fifth in the old First Division in Moores's first season as chairman, he was not satisfied. He decided that manager Johnny Carey had to go. Carey was duly informed after a meeting he and Moores had attended in London. It may have seemed a harsh decision, but it

Star recruits: Moores was responsible for bringing Harry Catterick (far left) to Everton, who in turn brought great success to the club. Roy Vernon (left) was one of his best buys. At Liverpool, Moores provided Bill Shankly with the opportunity to build a strong team that included the likes of Ian St John (right)

proved to be the right one. The man Moores chose as Carey's replacement was Harry Catterick, who had enjoyed considerable success as manager of Sheffield Wednesday. It was an inspired choice. Backed by Moores's money – he had made an interest-free loan of £56,000 available to buy players – Catterick plunged into the transfer market and brought a galaxy of stars to the club.

The first was Blackburn and Wales forward Roy Vernon. He was followed by Jimmy Gabriel from Dundee and Alex Young from Hearts. With this talent at his disposal, Catterick's team won the league title in 1962/63 and qualified for European competition in three consecutive seasons. In 1966 the FA Cup was won. In 1969/70, with the legendary trio of Ball, Harvey and Kendall as the engine of the side, the league title was secured again. But it wasn't just the trophies that Catterick won that earned him a place in the Everton hall of fame. He also built teams that played flowing football with amazing skill and flair, earning Everton the accolade 'The School of Science'.

MOORES STEPS DOWN AT EVERTON

Moores had two spells as Everton chairman. The first lasted until 1965 when he stepped down because of his wife Ruby's poor health. Just two months after his resignation, Ruby succumbed to cancer. The couple had been happily married for 42 years and it was a devastating blow for Moores. Despite his great loss, he remained on the board and continued

to serve the club faithfully. He had a second spell as chairman in the 1972/73 season but finally retired as a director in 1977 at the age of 81. However, long after his retirement, he remained Everton's biggest shareholder.

Moores was very generous with his money. During his 17 years as a director, he loaned the club vast sums interest free for team-building purposes. He also re-housed at his own expense families whose homes adjoining Goodison Park were demolished to make way for improved spectator accommodation before the 1966 World Cup. It was also thanks to John Moores that the great Dixie Dean did not sink into poverty as so many other footballers had done after quitting the game. Moores found him employment with the Littlewoods organisation and also arranged a testimonial match for him at Goodison Park on 7 April 1964. A crowd of nearly 37,000 saw a team of Everton and Liverpool Scottish players ('Liverton Scotland') defeat a team of Everton and Liverpool English players ('Liverton England') 3-1. The occasion raised about £7,000 for Dixie.

Everton's image as a club was also a matter of great concern to Moores. After a particularly hostile match against Stoke City he felt prompted to write the following strong words in a match programme:

'It is with the greatest regret that I, as chairman of Everton Football Club, have once more to appeal to that insignificant section of our

supporters who indulge in the vicious and dangerous practice of missile throwing to stop it or stay away away from Goodison Park!'

Moores once said: "If I wasn't so keen a football fan – just like the chaps on the terrace – I would never have got mixed up in it." Perhaps his passion for the game is best summed up in the words of George Orr, editor of the Everton fanzine *Blue Blood*:

'I for one think he was Mister Everton. I saw this multi-millionaire at many away games. He could have been anywhere in the world but you would see him on a cold and wet Saturday afternoon in Leicester or some other bleak ground. How many of you would be at an away game in the middle of an English winter if you were a millionaire?'

John Moores died at the age of 97 on 25 September 1993. This remarkable man will be remembered for his great achievements as a businessman, a patron of the arts and a supporter of charities. But at Goodison Park his magnificent contribution to the glorious period in Everton's history when the club became renowned as 'The School of Science' will be his enduring legacy.

BILL SHANKLY COMES TO ANFIELD

We have already seen that John Moores had great affection for Liverpool.

He watched the team on a regular basis, he financed the erection of two of the stands at Anfield, and he ignored the dividends from his shares in the club. But perhaps Liverpool supporters will be most grateful to him for the part he played in bringing the legendary Bill Shankly to Anfield and enabling Shankly to buy the players he wanted.

Moores was never in favour of the practice at Anfield of directors selecting the team. He firmly believed the manager alone should pick the team. With Liverpool languishing in the old Second Division in the latter half of the 1950s, Moores made this point to his friend, Tom Williams, chairman of Liverpool:

> "I told Tom they must go to someone who knows the game. They went to Matt Busby, and he recommended Bill Shankly to them. Bill had turned down Liverpool some years earlier, but now that he could pick the team, he accepted."

In December 1959 Shankly duly arrived. But it was another act of wisdom on Moores's part that gave Shankly the opportunities he needed to build his team. Moores had noticed that Liverpool's finances were not administered to good effect. For one thing, the board's ceiling of £12,000 on the purchase of a player restricted the quality of players that could be brought in. Moores suggested to Williams that the club would benefit from the expertise of Eric Sawyer (the managing director of Littlewoods) if he were appointed chairman of Liverpool's finance committee. Once again, Williams took his friend's advice.

It was a wise decision. Sawyer's breadth of vision and business acumen revitalised the club, enabling Shankly to lay the foundations of Liverpool's future greatness. On one occasion, when Shankly was keen to buy Ian St John from Motherwell, a Liverpool director, horrified at the asking price of £37,500, confronted Sawyer with the question: "Can we afford to buy him?" Without hesitation Sawyer replied: "Gentlemen we can't afford NOT to sign him." Thanks to Sawyer, Shankly was able to bring in the players he wanted and he never forgot the debt he owed him: "The triumphs came thanks to a man of vision, a director who would be associated only with success."

DAVID MOORES AND THE LIVERPOOL CONNECTION

When John Moores died in 1993, the family's links with Everton and Liverpool did not end. Moores bequeathed half his Liverpool shares to his nephew, David, and they couldn't have been placed in better hands. David was a passionate Liverpool supporter and as a youngster had given his team enthusiastic support from the Kop. He later even wore his heart on his car registration plate with its unmistakable number KOP 1.

It must have given him great pleasure to be elected in March 1990 to the board of directors of the club he so loved. Just over a year later, in August 1991, he became chairman, and as the majority shareholder owning almost 52% of the club, he had the major voice in its affairs. He remained at the helm for 16 years, a period in which the club enjoyed huge success, winning the European Champions League three times, the League Cup three times, the Super Cup twice, the UEFA Cup and the FA Cup.

In February 2007 Moores sold Liverpool to the Americans George Gillett Junior and Tom Hicks in the expectation of generating funds for the building of a new stadium in Stanley Park. Although he ceased to be the guiding hand at Anfield, Moores retained a seat on the board. His loyal service to Liverpool FC was recognised when the title of life president was conferred on him, thus perpetuating the family link with the club which stretches back almost 80 years.

Whether Blue or Red, there can be no doubt that the supporters of the city's two great clubs owe a great debt of gratitude to the family that has done so much to establish them as driving forces in English football and beyond. Trophy cabinets at Anfield and Goodison Park boasting a rich collection of silverware are a powerful reminder of the Moores family's legacy. These symbols of success are a tribute to their vision, energy and, above all, their passion for the clubs they loved and so faithfully served.

Family values: John Moores bequeathed half of his Liverpool shares to his nephew, David

A legend is born: John Moores was partly responsible for bringing Bill Shankly to Liverpool

CHAPTER 11
HILLSBOROUGH AND THE MILE OF SCARVES

15 April 1989 is a date no Liverpool supporter will ever forget. It was the day on which one of the worst disasters in football history occurred, and its memory remains as vivid and horrifying as ever. The occasion was the FA Cup semi-final clash between Liverpool and Nottingham Forest at the Hillsborough stadium in Sheffield, a match that should have been an exciting cup tie with the added spice of the prospect of an all-Merseyside final at Wembley. But it turned out to be a nightmare of the worst kind.

The day started normally enough. Liverpool and Nottingham Forest had both enjoyed good seasons and there was an air of eager anticipation as both sets of supporters made their way to the ground in glorious sunshine. As the Liverpool supporters headed for the Leppings Lane end of the ground there was nothing at first to suggest a terrible tragedy was about to unfold. But about half an hour before kick-off, the congestion at the turnstiles had built to such an alarming level that supporters had become frightened and distressed. To relieve the pressure at the turnstiles, the police took the decision to open one of the exit gates in the perimeter wall. The consequences proved disastrous.

Within minutes of the gate being opened, some 2,000 Liverpool fans made their way onto the terrace, most going down a tunnel immediately in front of them. The tunnel led to two already full pens but they had no idea of this. As they pushed forward into the pens, the crush at the front by the perimeter fencing became intolerable for those unfortunate enough to be there. There was no means of escape. As the pressure from behind increased, many lost consciousness. Tragically, 96 never recovered.

The shock and horror of the disaster reverberated throughout Britain and far beyond, but nowhere more so than on Merseyside, which was engulfed with grief. It was a grief of such intensity that it could not be carried alone. Its burden had to be shared. And instinctively Anfield became the place to share it.

LIVERPOOL AND EVERTON UNITED IN GRIEF

That same night the Shankly Gates were adorned with flowers, but what had been a comparative trickle of people on the Saturday became a flood on Sunday as thousands made their way to Anfield. Partisan loyalties were immediately forgotten as Everton supporters rallied round their Liverpool counterparts to share their pain and sorrow. It was a city united in grief.

The ground was opened to the public and very quickly the goal in front of the Kop was bedecked with floral tributes and scarves. But they were not only in the red of Liverpool but also the blue of Everton. Along the

United: The mile of scarves is carried through Anfield to the Kop, 22 April 1989

crossbar was a red scarf tied to a blue one with a poppy attached to the knot. On the ground just in front of the goalmouth a little girl had placed a bunch of flowers and laid her blue and white scarf on it with the message: 'To all the boys who died. From Rachel, an Everton fan.' There were also wooden shields of both clubs tied side by side. On one the message read: 'We should have been at Wembley together, but today we are together in grief.' Liverpool manager Kenny Dalglish admitted the next day that he had wept at the sight of Liverpool and Everton supporters paying their tributes together. He said: "It was both the saddest and the most beautiful thing I have ever seen."

Anfield remained open for the whole of the following week, from 9am until 7.30pm, and it is estimated that up to two million people came to pay their respects. But it was always noticeable that countless Everton supporters were among the mourners. At the Anfield Road end of the ground, where Evertonians stood to support their team on derby days, the goal was decked out in blue and white scarves in honour of the dead.

When Labour Party leader Neil Kinnock came to Anfield to pay his tributes, he was hugged by an emotional Liverpool fan who pleaded with him: "Tell the country the truth about Liverpool." An Evertonian, standing close by, added: "Blue and red together Neil, tell them that." As Kinnock looked across the pitch covered with flowers, he replied: "You only have to look here to see there's almost as much blue as red. That's what counts." And he promised he would tell the House of Commons what he had seen at Anfield.

EVERTON'S SEMI-FINAL VICTORY OVERSHADOWED
While the tragic events at Hillsborough were unfolding, Everton were engaged in a semi-final contest with Norwich City at Villa Park in Birmingham. The joy of their 1-0 victory over the Canaries that took them to Wembley was instantly dispelled as the terrible news from Hillsborough filtered through. Manager Colin Harvey and his players were deeply shocked and Pat Nevin, who scored the decisive goal, refused to discuss the match with reporters. His only thoughts were for the bereaved, and he was eloquent in his expressions of sympathy for them.

The Everton supporters in the coaches leaving Villa Park were also in sombre mood. One of them summed up his feelings in a letter to the *Liverpool Echo* three days later. It was headed "Just a gesture from an Evertonian" and is reproduced here in abbreviated form:

> *'Three of us, all Evertonians, were out for a semi-final eve celebration. We were with another friend, a Liverpudlian. The sense of camaraderie and conviviality did the soul good... We were off to Villa, the Reds were off to Hillsborough... The coaches arrived. Reds here, Blues there.*

> *[At the end of the game against Norwich] our whistle went. We had done it! Yes! Nevin got chaired off.*

> *'As we filed out, we heard it... The news spread like wildfire... We all knew somebody there. All of us... The radio on the coach told us. Pat Nevin told us. A very sombre coach indeed. Then 15 miles from home, we saw the first Liverpool coach. I've never felt so guilty about wearing a blue scarf all my life.'*

It was signed: 'With deepest sympathy, from Someone Blue.'

For Everton supporters, Wembley was the furthest thing from their minds. They only had thoughts for friends and loved ones who may have been at Hillsborough. Many waited anxiously with Reds' fans at Lime Street Station as the first trains arrived home from Sheffield that night.

Everton immediately postponed their Central League home games against Derby County reserves and Derby's first team that were due to be played that week. They would also have called off their match against Tottenham Hotspur the following Saturday, but it was away and had to be played. Supporters who did travel to Tottenham were subdued, still numb from the shock of Hillsborough. There was no chanting and no cheering. The only expressions of emotion were warm applause, first when the Tannoy announced music would not be played for birthday requests, then when floral tributes were laid, and finally after the minute's silence to remember those who had died.

In the aftermath of the tragedy Kenny Dalglish and his Liverpool players did all they could to help the injured and bereaved, talking to fans, visiting hospitals and attending funerals. It was a massive emotional strain for them, and Blues boss Colin Harvey was quick to offer his support:

> *'It goes without saying that my players will do anything they can to help. Whether it's simply a matter of talking to the fans or attending funerals, we will be only too willing to play our part.'*

RED AND BLUE AT LIVERPOOL'S CATHEDRALS
Although Anfield became the main focus for the supporters' grief, Liverpool's two cathedrals also played a very important part in providing comfort. On the Sunday evening after the disaster, thousands flocked to the Roman Catholic Metropolitan Cathedral to attend a Requiem Mass. As the cathedral could only accommodate 3,000, another service had to be held for the 5,000 outside.

The service was led by the Archbishop of Liverpool, the Most Rev Derek Worlock, but he was joined by the Anglican Bishop of Liverpool, the

Time to reflect: Kenny Dalglish with his wife and daughter at the memorial service for the Hillsborough victims in the Anglican Cathedral (top). A Requiem Mass was held at the Roman Catholic cathedral (above) on the Sunday after the tragedy

Right Rev David Sheppard and the Free Church Moderator, Rev Dr John Newton. David Sheppard, although a former England cricketer, was a keen football fan and regularly watched Everton and Liverpool play. He had been away on holiday with his family in the Outer Hebrides but had been hurriedly transported back to Liverpool by helicopter in time for the Mass.

It was an emotional service and it struck a chord when Archbishop Worlock told the congregation: "The tragedy of Hillsborough has brought Liverpool to its knees – not in defeat but in prayer." Looking around the congregation, he noticed the Liverpool and Everton players, Liverpool and Everton supporters wearing their scarves, and youngsters in replica Liverpool and Everton kits. With a smile he told them: "Thank you for being the marvellous people you are."

After the service, Everton manager Colin Harvey spoke of the deep bond between the clubs:

> "We are not a divided city. There are Evertonians and Liverpudlians in the same family. It was always going to be an occasion when we would come together and help each other. We reached Wembley on Saturday, but our feelings went from absolute elation to the very opposite when we heard what had happened."

A fortnight later, on Saturday 29 April at 11am, a special memorial service was held in Liverpool's Anglican Cathedral. It was led by Bishop Sheppard with the assistance of Archbishop Worlock and Dr John Newton. The Anglican Archbishop of York, the Most Rev John Habgood, and the Roman Catholic Archbishop of Westminster, Cardinal Basil Hume, also took part. In the congregation were Prime Minister Margaret Thatcher and the leader of the opposition, Neil Kinnock.

The 2,000 seats inside the cathedral were mostly allocated to the bereaved families, but giant television screens relayed the one-hour service to more than 8,000 people who had gathered outside the cathedral. Millions more watched on TV.

Among the first to arrive were the Liverpool and Everton teams, led by their managers Kenny Dalglish and Colin Harvey. Once again, the numerous Liverpool and Everton scarves in the cathedral showed the deep bond between the two clubs. This was never more evident than the poignant moment when the Books of Condolence with thousands of expressions of sympathy were carried to the altar by Everton supporter Andy McGrory and Liverpool supporter David Lynan. Dr Newton was moved to give thanks for the city's "profound sense of unity in grief".

THE MILE OF SCARVES

The bonds between Everton and Liverpool were much in evidence in the immediate aftermath of Hillsborough but there was no symbol more powerful of their unity than 'The Mile of Scarves'.

It was the brainchild of two Liverpool cab drivers, Jimmy Plunkett (28) and Tony Atkinson (26) who wanted to pay tribute to those who had died by forming a one-mile chain of Everton and Liverpool scarves linking Goodison Park and Anfield. As Jimmy explained: "I thought up the idea because it was a way of linking the two grounds and the supporters."

Their initial estimate was that 2,500 would be needed for 'The Chain of Unity', but it turned out to be 4,000. An appeal went out to fans to donate their scarves and a special 'scarfmobile' toured Merseyside to collect them.

The response was enthusiastic and the required number was soon collected. The first scarf was tied to the gates of Goodison Park by Everton star Ian Snodin and from there the chain continued out of Bullens Road, over Walton Road, across Stanley Park and through the Bill Shankly Memorial Gates at Anfield to the Kop. On Saturday 22 April a moving ceremony led by Archbishop Worlock and Bishop Sheppard was held at Anfield for the tying of the final scarf to the Kop. It was attended by thousands, including the players of Everton, Liverpool and Tranmere Rovers.

The lengthy line was greeted with a deafening cheer on its arrival at Anfield where it was carried along the perimeter track to the Kop. At exactly 3.06pm, the time the game had been stopped the previous week at Hillsborough, a minute's silence was observed to remember those who had died. At 3.07pm, while Bishop Sheppard read the 'Lord's Prayer', Liverpool's Peter Beardsley and Everton's Ian Snodin joined hands with Barry Devonshire, whose 18-year-old son Chris had died at Hillsborough, to tie the final scarf to the Kop. As one Liverpool fan wrote later: 'It was a show of unity that incited such intense pride in the midst of such distress.'

It was not only in Liverpool that there was such a clear show of unity. At the London Marathon the next day, crowds lining the 26-mile course were moved to tears and broke into spontaneous applause as 250 Merseysiders wearing Liverpool and Everton strips ran the distance together singing 'You'll Never Walk Alone'. Outpourings of love such as this helped make the pain of Hillsborough just a little easier to bear.

Show of support: Blues' boss Colin Harvey

Mile end: Peter Beardsley and Ian Snodin join up with Barry Devonshire to tie the final scarf to the Kop

CHAPTER 12
THE SPIRIT OF THE WEMBLEY DERBIES

Since Everton and Liverpool's first-ever encounter on Saturday 22 April 1893 in the final of the Liverpool Senior Cup, they have contested more than 200 derby matches. These games have always been fiercely competitive and provided their supporters with enough memories and stories to fill several books. But of all the derby games between the clubs, three have a unique place in Merseyside folklore because they were played on the greatest football stage in England – Wembley. The first was the League Cup final of 1984. It was followed by the FA Cup finals of 1986 and 1989. With millions of TV viewers across the globe watching these intriguing contests between fierce local rivals, the teams and their supporters were under the microscope as never before. What kind of face did they present to the world? This chapter gives the answer.

THE 1984 LEAGUE CUP – 'THE FRIENDLY FINAL'

There was much at stake in this first Wembley meeting between the Blues and the Reds. For one thing, it was not known how the rival fans would behave. Violence had marred many cup finals in previous years, and it was feared the same might happen again. Clearly the reputation of the two clubs, as well as the city of Liverpool, was on the line.

There was also much at stake on the playing side. Liverpool were chasing a league and League Cup double, and were poised to retain the latter trophy permanently if they won the match. Although they had won the League Cup competition for the previous three years, only the last two tournaments had been sponsored by the Milk Marketing Board. This particular cup – the 'Milk Cup' as it was known – was Liverpool's to keep if they won it for the third year in succession. Significantly, it would also give the Reds' new manager, Joe Fagan, his first trophy, a massive boost for the man who had just succeeded the hugely successful Bob Paisley.

For Everton, too, it was a golden opportunity to land a coveted double. They were due to meet Watford in the FA Cup final a month later, and victory over Liverpool would put them in a strong position to achieve this. However, they would not find Liverpool easy. The Reds had just won the old Division One title for the third successive year and were at the peak of their form.

One person who would have loved to see this Wembley derby was legendary Liverpool manager Bill Shankly. Before the match, Syd McGuiness, chairman of the Everton Supporters' Club, told the *Football Echo*:

'I only wish Bill Shankly was alive to see this match. When he retired

Friendly Final: While the 1984 Milk Cup final was competitive, the mood was amicable between the sides, as can be seen in this joint team photograph (left)

Merseyside united: Peter Reid from Everton (left) and Alan Kennedy from Liverpool embrace after the final whistle in 1984

Right: The teams went on a combined lap of honour

he used to pop into Bellefield [Everton's training camp] quite a lot because his house was just around the corner. Bill always spoke about his dream of an all-Merseyside final.'

THE FAMILY ATMOSPHERE
When the big day arrived – Sunday 25 March – many thousands of Merseysiders headed for London. Lime Street Station was awash with colour as countless fans sporting blue and red filed into 20 special trains, but it was the motorway that provided the most remarkable sights. Blue and red scarves were regularly spotted streaming from the same vehicle, easing fears that there might be trouble between the rival supporters. The players were deeply impressed by this display of unity. Everton's John Bailey summed up their feelings perfectly:

"Driving down the motorway there were loads of cars with blue scarves out of one side and red out of the other... It was fabulous the way they all mixed. It had never been seen before."

The team line-ups for this historic occasion were:
Everton: Neville Southall; Gary Stevens, Derek Mountfield, Kevin Ratcliffe, John Bailey; Kevin Sheedy (Alan Harper 76 mins), Peter Reid, Kevin Richardson, Alan Irvine; Adrian Heath, Graeme Sharp.

Liverpool: Bruce Grobbelaar; Phil Neal, Mark Lawrenson, Alan Hansen, Alan Kennedy; Sammy Lee, Graeme Souness, Ronnie Whelan; Kenny Dalglish, Ian Rush, Craig Johnston (Michael Robinson 90 mins)

They provided the 100,000 spectators and the huge TV audience with a football feast. It was one of the most exciting matches seen at Wembley in years. The game was played at a furious pace, and the non-stop action had everything but a goal, but it was the spirit in which it was contested that made the biggest impression. On the pitch, the teams gave their all in an energy-sapping contest but their sportsmanship was outstanding. It was matched by an equally good spirit in the stands and on the terraces as supporters of different persuasions mingled freely in an atmosphere of friendship and good humour.

After a gruelling two hours of football the exhausted players joined together in a combined lap of honour, providing the cue for their supporters to break out in the spontaneous chant of "Merseyside, Merseyside, Merseyside". It is no wonder this game was dubbed 'The

Friendly Final'. The famous old stadium had never seen anything like it before. Even after the match, the good spirit continued as husbands and wives, brothers and sisters, groups of friends – all in a mix of blue and red – strolled happily down Wembley Way to Wembley Park Station where the joyful chant "Merseyside la-la-la" summed up the mood of the day.

Brian Clough, the controversial manager of Nottingham Forest, said afterwards that it was not only a great advertisement for football but also "a tribute to the city of Liverpool". His words were echoed by many others. One fan told a *Liverpool Echo* reporter: 'I wonder just how many people watching on telly all over the world realise that something like this could only happen in a city like Liverpool. I'm a Red, me mate's an Evertonian. I think he's crazy, but here we are side by side.'

Commander Alan Gibson, in charge of Wembley security, commented: "It was, as I had hoped, a great family occasion. One father I spoke to had two sons with him supporting Everton and Liverpool. It was that sort of day."

The last word belongs to the Queen Mother, the principal guest of honour at the game. She simply said: "What a lovely, happy occasion."

'THE FRIENDLY FINAL' – REPLAY AT MAINE ROAD

The replay at Maine Road, Manchester, the following Wednesday echoed the Wembley spirit in every way. The unity and good humour characteristic of the previous Sunday were just as evident, with blue and red scarves fluttering from the same cars as many Everton and Liverpool supporters travelled together to the match. The mutual goodwill between the supporters was further symbolised by the sight of the Everton Toffee Lady happily chatting to Liverpool fans, a sure sign that this was going to be another occasion with a strong family atmosphere.

The Liverpool line-up was unchanged from Sunday, while in the Everton team Alan Harper replaced Kevin Sheedy. Andy King came on for Alan Irvine in the 70th minute.

The crowd of 52,000 had plenty to excite them. Once again the game was fast and furious, both sides giving their all. But it was Liverpool who had the edge, and a magnificent 21st-minute goal by man of the match Graeme Souness was enough to secure a permanent place for the Milk Cup in the Anfield trophy room and give manager Joe Fagan his first major success. The spirit of the occasion was demonstrated by the tremendous ovation the Everton supporters gave the victorious Liverpool team.

Commenting afterwards on the atmosphere at Maine Road, Everton's John Bailey told the local press: 'The reaction of both sets of supporters was tremendous at the final whistle. The "Merseyside" chant went up again and I was in tears.'

He had every reason to be moved.

THE 1986 FA CUP FINAL – A MERSEYSIDE CARNIVAL

1985/86 had been a magnificent season for both Everton and Liverpool. The Reds had narrowly pipped the Blues to the championship of the old First Division, reversing the order of the previous year when Everton took the title. And now they had both earned a place in the FA Cup final at Wembley. Would Liverpool win the coveted double and leave Everton without a trophy, or could Everton salvage their season by taking the cup home with them?

Without their dependable keeper, Neville Southall, who was sidelined with injury, Everton would not find it easy. His replacement, Bobby Simms, had just returned from a loan period with Notts County in the old Third Division and had only played 10 first-team games for Everton. Meanwhile, Liverpool player-manager Kenny Dalglish, who had been named Bell's Manager of the Year, was making his 900th appearance as a professional footballer. He was also to make history as the first player-manager at Wembley.

Blues' manager Howard Kendall also took his place in the record books, equalling former Arsenal manager Terry Neill's feat in taking a team to three successive cup finals.

BLUES AND REDS TOGETHER

The incredible family atmosphere of the 1984 Wembley derby was repeated in 1986. On Saturday 10 May a convoy of 26,000 supporters travelling in 400 coaches were joined on the motorway by fleets of minibuses and cars, while a further 8,000 headed for London on 19 special trains from Lime Street. The mix of blue and red in the same vehicles showed the marvellous spirit between the fans.

On arrival in London there was a carnival atmosphere as rival fans linked arms and sauntered happily along together singing: "Here we go." At Paddington Underground station one ticket collector remarked: "This place is one of the worst flashpoint areas and working here on a matchday can be a nightmare. But not today. It was sheer pleasure."

The team line-ups were:
Everton: Bobby Mimms; Gary Stevens (Adrian Heath 71 mins), Derek Mountfield, Kevin Ratcliffe, Pat Van Den Hauwe; Trevor Steven, Peter Reid,

Paul Bracewell, Kevin Sheedy; Gary Lineker, Graeme Sharp.

Liverpool: Bruce Grobbelaar; Steve Nicol, Mark Lawrenson, Alan Hansen, Jim Beglin; Craig Johnston, Jan Molby, Kevin MacDonald, Ronnie Whelan; Kenny Dalglish, Ian Rush.

This was the match that had everything – drama, excitement, skill and four brilliant goals. It was Everton's Gary Lineker, England's Footballer of the Year, who opened the scoring, taking his tally for the season to 40. But his spectacular goal was cancelled out in the second half by Ian Rush. It was an ominous omen because Liverpool had never lost a match in which Rush scored. And that was a total of 120 matches. Sure enough, Craig Johnston gave Liverpool the lead five minutes later and the match was sealed when Rush added his second six minutes from time.

The spirit in the crowd was as marvellous as that on the pitch. Blues and Reds mingled good-naturedly together, and at the end of the match, as the weary Everton players did a lap of honour, the chant "Merseyside, Merseyside, Merseyside" rang around the ground. The senior police officer at Wembley paid a well-deserved tribute to the fans: "It was a good-humoured crowd inside the stadium. I only wish that all football fans could

Four-goal thriller: 1985 Player of the Year Gary Lineker (far left with trophy) celebrates putting Everton ahead in the 1986 FA Cup final (left), but Everton's joy was short-lived. Above: Ian Rush scores his second goal, and Liverpool's third, in the 3-1 win

behave that way. The atmosphere was very friendly with a total mix of fans." And the Merseysiders themselves were obviously aware of this unique spirit when they unashamedly proclaimed: "Are you watching, Manchester?"

After the match the carnival continued. In Trafalgar Square Everton supporters, showing no signs of a deflated spirit, leapt joyously into the fountains with Liverpool supporters. One of the Liverpool fans remarked: "People around here just cannot believe that we are celebrating together. But they don't know us. If Liverpool and Everton fans are together there will never be any trouble.'

PARADING THE TROPHY
Half a million people turned out in Liverpool the next day to welcome the returning heroes. But the reception was not reserved for the cup winners alone. Everton, too, had their share of the glory. On arrival at Liverpool airport in the same plane, the teams boarded two open-top buses for a parade round the jubilant city. In a magnificent sporting gesture, Everton were invited to lead the procession.

Kenny Dalglish, amazed at the sight of Everton and Liverpool fans

celebrating together along the 18-mile route through Liverpool, said: "To see so many Blues fans made it extra special. The friendship between the supporters is incredible and does not happen anywhere else. The supporters are a credit to themselves, and a credit to the clubs and British football." But the players, too, shared a special bond. Liverpool's Ian Rush was quick to spare a thought for the defeated Everton players: "It is a pity that someone had to lose, but some of the Everton lads are my best mates and always will be."

1989 – THE HILLSBOROUGH CUP FINAL
No meeting between Everton and Liverpool could possibly have been more poignant than the FA Cup final of 1989. It took place less than a month after the tragic disaster at the Hillsborough stadium in Sheffield on

Saturday 15 April when Liverpool met Nottingham Forest in the semi-final. That day the terrible crush in the Leppings Lane end of the ground cost 96 Liverpool supporters their lives. Liverpool and Everton had pulled together after the tragedy and given help wherever they could, and it somehow seemed right that they should meet at Wembley. In the words of Liverpool manager Kenny Dalglish: "Having an all-Merseyside FA Cup final is a fairy tale after all that has happened."

On the football side, Liverpool were targeting another league/FA Cup double after missing out the previous year when Wimbledon dashed their hopes at Wembley. They were also hoping to break the jinx of having the Footballer of the Year in their side. In the four previous seasons, the FA Cup final was lost by the side fielding the holder of this award. This year it was Liverpool's Steve Nicol.

The number of fans heading for Wembley was huge: some 70,000 made the journey by car, train, coach and air. As before, many vehicles proudly displayed blue and red as families and friends of different allegiance travelled together.

There was a poignant atmosphere in the ceremony preceding the match. Before Gerry Marsden sang Liverpool's anthem 'You'll Never Walk Alone', he told the crowd:

> "I came here to sing this song for three reasons. First for the 95 who died at Hillsborough [another died later], secondly for those lads injured who couldn't be here and are watching at home on television, and thirdly for the Evertonians and the Liverpudlians who helped us after that terrible disaster. All I can say is Merseyside showed to the world just how great we are. Merseyside United!"

And the sight of red and blue scarves held aloft in the crowd of nearly 83,000 during the singing confirmed the feeling of togetherness.

A WEMBLEY THRILLER
As with the previous Wembley derbies, this was a game of passion, drama and excitement. Representing Everton were:

Neville Southall, Neil McDonald, Pat Van Den Hauwe, Kevin Ratcliffe, Dave Watson, Paul Bracewell (Stuart McCall 59 mins), Pat Nevin, Trevor Steven, Graeme Sharp, Tony Cottee and Kevin Sheedy (Ian Wilson 74 mins).

Facing them in the Liverpool line-up were:

Bruce Grobbelaar, Gary Ablett, Steve Staunton (Barry Venison 90 mins), Steve Nicol, Ronnie Whelan, Alan Hansen, Peter Beardsley, John Aldridge (Ian Rush 72 mins), Ray Houghton, John Barnes and Steve McMahon.

Liverpool were quick off the mark, John Aldridge scoring after only four minutes. For most of the game it looked as if this might be the winner. However, Everton scored a last-gasp equaliser through Stuart McCall to send the game into extra time. Within minutes of the re-start, Ian Rush restored Liverpool's lead with a powerful shot to beat Dixie Dean's record of 19 derby goals. Again McCall equalised but it was Rush who finally clinched victory for Liverpool with a superb header.

It was a marvellous game played in a great spirit. The fans displayed good humour and camaraderie throughout, Blues standing shoulder-to-shoulder with Reds as if it were the most natural thing in the world. This spirit of togetherness impressed Liverpool 'keeper Bruce Grobbelaar on his journey home:

> "When we were driving up the motorway, the Everton fans were leaning out of their sunroofs clapping us. It is something you would never get in any other city in the world, the losers cheering the winners. Merseyside is a unique place."

The following day was one of celebration as thousands of Merseysiders, Reds and Blues together, lined a 13-mile route in glorious sunshine to applaud the cup winners. It was a wonderful tonic after the sorrow of the past few weeks.

Looking around the vast crowds, Kenny Dalglish remarked: "You like to think you can help people. That's what probably makes this better than some of the other wins. If we've done anything to make it better for people after Hillsborough we are delighted." His wife Marina expressed the feelings of the players: "They won this trophy for the bereaved families."

It was a fitting finale to a magnificent weekend. As a Liverpool supporter wrote in the *Daily Post* a few days later: 'It was a great weekend, and I thank the Evertonians for making it so. It was a joy to be with them.' The same sentiment, echoed by Peter Oldham in the same paper, provides a fitting conclusion to this chapter:

> 'Where else in Europe do rival fans come to matches in the same coaches? Where else do they sit side by side in the stadium? Where else do they applaud each other's team on and off the field? The most enduring memory for me will be the sight of policemen looking on bemused as scores of Blues and Reds supporters danced together below Wembley Way, joyously chanting not the name of their teams, but "Merseyside... Merseyside... Merseyside".'

Southall beats
Aldridge to the
ball in the 1989
FA Cup final

CHAPTER 13
RHYS JONES AND 'Z-CARS' AT ANFIELD

Wednesday, 22 August 2007. It was a warm summer's evening as bright, bubbly 11-year-old Rhys Jones made his way home from another enjoyable training session in Croxteth Park with his friends of the Fir Tree Boys Football Club in Liverpool. It was not far to walk, just a few hundred yards. But tragically he never reached home. As he crossed the car park of the Fir Tree public house, he was struck down by a bullet fired by a hooded gunman intent on killing members of a rival gang. Rhys had innocently wandered into the line of fire. He died minutes later in the arms of his mother who had rushed to the scene. A short, promising, young life had been cruelly and senselessly snatched away.

Rhys Jones was a happy, fun-loving, outgoing youngster with a captivating, cheeky grin. His greatest passion was football and he was an ardent Everton fan. The senseless killing of such a cheerful young boy stunned Merseyside and sent shock waves throughout the country. People were horrified by his death and moved with compassion for his family. There was also deeply felt anger at the gun and gang culture that was taking hold in many cities, and out of the anger grew a fierce determination to bring it to an end.

Hearts went out to Rhys's parents, Stephen and Melanie, and to his older brother, Owen. People did all they could to offer help and support. Three days after his death, Rhys's beloved Everton reached out to the family, warmly receiving Stephen, Melanie and Owen as their special guests for the match against Blackburn Rovers. Before kick-off they were taken onto the pitch where they stood between Everton manager, David Moyes, and Blackburn manager, Mark Hughes, as tribute was paid to Rhys with a minute's applause from the crowd. Poignantly, Everton winger James McFadden dedicated his equalising goal to the youngster.

The club paid further tribute to Rhys on 27 August when the entire Everton squad visited the scene of his killing, placing mementoes at the spot where he died. Mikel Arteta, Andrew Johnson and Joseph Yobo – Rhys's favourite players – left their shirts from the Blackburn match while Tim Cahill left a pair of boots. A wreath in the shape of a blue and white football was also placed among the mementoes.

'Z-CARS' AT ANFIELD

Liverpool FC, Everton's fierce local rivals, also responded to the tragedy but in a way that was both remarkable and unexpected. Tony Barrett, features writer for the *Liverpool Echo*, had suggested on his blog the day after Rhys's death that 'Johnny Todd', the theme tune of the TV series 'Z-Cars', should be played at Anfield as a tribute to Rhys. As 'Z-Cars' is the tune to which the Everton team runs out at Goodison Park, it was a controversial suggestion. Barrett was well aware that relationships between Everton and Liverpool supporters had been strained in recent years and he knew he had to justify his proposal:

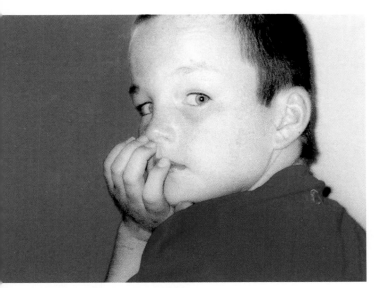

Moved to tears: Rhys Jones's parents Melanie (centre) and Stephen (right), stand with their elder son Owen as the Everton football club anthem – 'Z-Cars' – is played at Anfield

'He may have been a bluenose but he was one of us – a lad from Liverpool who lived for his football. His family deserve our solidarity and I can think of no better way of showing it than putting our traditional football rivalries to one side if only for one night and playing the one song that meant the world to him... I haven't forgotten the solidarity that was shown to us by ordinary Everton fans in the aftermath of Hillsborough, and this is our chance to repay the favour to at least one family of ordinary Evertonians in their darkest hour. I know this is controversial and I know there will be those of you who think I'm talking nonsense but just think of the message doing something like this would send out to the rest of the world.'

But the response from Liverpool supporters was amazing. Many contacted the club and the *Echo*, urging that the 'Z-Cars' theme should be played at Anfield. There were many positive postings on websites, the two below being typical:

'Great idea, as a lifelong red (Kop S/T holder for most of my life) and resident on the Croxteth Park estate, I would certainly back this idea. Football rivalry needs to be put to one side at times like this, and I hope LFC will certainly do something to show solidarity with the blues. It could have been anyone's child, any of us in that car park and I don't think your idea is as controversial as it sounds.'

'What a lovely idea Tony. I was born and bred to be a red just like little Rhys a blue, but in time of trouble we as a city stand up as a city together, and united we stand.'

Everton fans were just as aware of the significance of Barrett's suggestion:

'As a blue, just the thought of you lot doing this for us is making me well up. If you do it, it'll not be forgotten.'

'As a mad blue I think your idea is really good. When my mates died at Hillsborough I sang 'You'll Never Walk Alone' for them and all reds.'

Liverpool chief executive Rick Parry discussed the proposal with the Jones family who were delighted at the idea. It was agreed that 'Z-Cars' would be played prior to the start of Liverpool's European Champions League qualifier against Toulouse on Tuesday 28 August.

Rhys's uncle, Neil Jones, confessed that the family had been overwhelmed by the magnificent gesture of support from the club. He said:

"When I told them about the proposed tribute at Anfield, Melanie

said playing 'Johnny Todd' at Anfield would be a unique event, a complete one-off, just like Rhys, and a fitting tribute to him as it was his favourite tune. She's also pretty sure he'll have a little mischievous grin on his face at the thought of being the cause of it."

Any doubts Rhys's parents and brother may have had about the reception they would get when they stepped onto the pitch at Anfield in their Everton colours were quickly dispelled. They received an emotional and heartfelt welcome from the thousands of Reds' supporters in the ground. When Reds' legend Brian Hall announced over the tannoy that Everton's anthem was to be played in memory of Rhys, the crowd broke into spontaneous applause. They then listened in respectful silence as the music was played. After the anthems of both clubs had been played, there was a minute's applause by players and fans as a tribute to Rhys. Reds' manager Rafa Benitez then came up to Stephen, Melanie and Owen and embraced them in turn. The warmth of the support the family had received at Anfield that evening left an indelible impression on Melanie:

"It is the people in this city that make it special – in our minds there is no other place like it where the people feel your pain and sorrow. The football fans at Anfield who clapped us when 'Z-Cars' was played and put their arms around us have shown that."

It also deeply impressed countless other Evertonians. The following selection of website postings is just a sample of the many positive responses that appeared:

'Tremendous gesture by Liverpool Football Club and I commend them totally for it... Well done Liverpool and their fans, from an appreciative Blue.'

'I am a die hard Evertonian but all banter and slagging aside this shows class as a football club and as human beings. I commend yourself and LFC for this heartfelt show of support and the class the club has shown. Thank you.'

'Liverpool. Bloody typical! Just when you love hating them, they go and do something like this: they're going to play "Z-Cars" at Anfield tonight in response to requests from their fans in tribute to Rhys Jones. Nice touch. Fair play to them.'

'Well done to Liverpool for this gesture and for responding to the wishes of their fans. It is great to see football used as a unifying force instead of just an excuse for an argument or a fight as it is by some people.'

Warm welcome:
Liverpool manager
Rafael Benitez greets
the Jones family

'It's not about red or blue tonight, it's about remembering the life of a child whose life was ended all too early. Hopefully his family will draw some comfort from the show of unity from two groups of fans who seem to grow more hostile each season.'

'Glad the club listened to the fans and did this. Well done, Tony. Fabulous idea and you deserve credit for proposing it. This will hopefully ease tensions between the rival fans which has become silly over recent seasons.'

'What a fantastic touch by Liverpool FC tonight, playing that song in their ground as a tribute to Rhys Jones. It has always saddened me how the derbies have degenerated into outright hatred. I hope this can be the start of a friendlier rivalry like in the past.'

Tony Barrett, writing in the *Echo* the next day, summed up the significance of the occasion:

'In death little Rhys Jones has achieved something so incredible that it will never, ever be forgotten — he has united Merseyside once again.'

BLUES AND REDS UNITE AT RHYS'S FUNERAL

The unity shown at Anfield was repeated at Rhys's funeral, which took place at the Anglican cathedral on 6 September. Two hours before the cortege was due to pass Goodison Park, hundreds had begun to line the streets near the ground to pay their respects. Many Liverpool fans were among them. One placed a single blue rose at the base of Dixie Dean's statue with the simple message: 'In loving memory of Rhys. Rest in Peace from a Liverpool supporter.'

When the cortege arrived at the cathedral there were large crowds outside waiting to pay their respects, some wearing blue, others red. The blue and red mix was also prominent inside the building where 1,800 had congregated. Some Liverpool fans had even chosen to wear blue scarves as an expression of solidarity with the Jones family. And, of course, players from both clubs were there, too.

Rhys's uncle Neil Jones, in his tribute to his nephew, emphasised that Rhys had had a healthy perspective of the rivalry between the clubs:

> *"He was football crazy, absolutely nuts about it and his team was Everton FC. As his Red uncle, it was my duty to rib him about being a bluenose, but his belief was unshakable. Football is nothing without rivalry, particularly in a city such as ours. Some of Rhys's closest friends are here wearing shirts of a different colour but he always saw beyond that. They were friends first and football rivals second."*

RHYS JONES COMMUNITY CENTRE
Rhys's death had been the catalyst for a new spirit of goodwill among thousands of Everton and Liverpool supporters, but it also galvanised the city into action against the growing gun and gang culture. Some very important initiatives were launched in a determined effort to counteract it. Rhys's own local community was quick off the mark, with the Croxteth Country Park Residents' Association setting up the Rhys Jones Memorial Fund.

Its aim was to raise enough money to build a community centre bearing Rhys's name. The centre would serve as "a catalyst to bring together our community, both young and old", and would include sports facilities such as all-weather soccer pitches. Both Everton and Liverpool declared their support for the project.

LIVERPOOL UNITES: BLUES AND REDS TOGETHER
In the wake of Rhys's tragic death, the *Liverpool Echo* launched a major campaign on 28 September 2007 with the purpose of providing a channel for the people of Liverpool to lobby Parliament with a view to changing the existing gun laws. The symbol of the campaign (which is ongoing), is a purple ribbon, the colour that results when blue is mixed with red. The choice of colour was inspired by the unity displayed by Everton and Liverpool fans in their support for the Jones family. Thousands of purple ribbons and wristbands were produced for people to wear as a tribute to Rhys and as a demonstration of support for the campaign. Another aim of the campaign was to raise £100,000 towards the cost of building the Rhys Jones Community Centre.

Everton and Liverpool football clubs immediately pledged their support.

Blues' manager David Moyes said: "The *Echo* campaign should be supported by everyone who desires a safer world. I know I speak for every single member of my first-team squad when I say that gun crime is a modern evil." Reds' boss Rafael Benitez expressed similar sentiments: "Having recently met the family of young Rhys Jones, I fully understand the absolute misery which gun crime can bring to a normal decent family. I will wear my ribbon to show my support for them and I hope that many other people do the same."

Speaking on behalf of the Liverpool players, Jamie Carragher said: "All the lads are delighted to support the campaign in Rhys Jones's name. As soon as we got the ribbons we put them on straightaway for training because we know how important it is to show solidarity with Rhys's family. One of the best things about this city is that the people pull together when it matters most, and this is one of those times."

Everton and Liverpool also gave their wholehearted support to the Rhys Jones Memorial Cup, a tournament launched in May 2008 for under-12s (boys and girls). Rhys's father, Stephen, explained that the purpose of the tournament was to give youngsters the chance to play at Everton and Liverpool's prestigious academies and also to get the message across to children to join a team not a gang.

CONCERT, WALK AND RUN FOR RHYS
On Friday 15 August 2008 a star-studded concert was held at the Liverpool Echo Arena to raise funds towards the cost of building the Rhys Jones Community Centre. The Concert for Rhys was the idea of Kate Mayers and Sarah Doughty, two friends of Melanie Jones. They approached the *Liverpool Echo*, who recruited Lyn Staunton of Power Promotions to line up star acts. The event was a huge success. £50,000 was raised and the 8,000-plus crowd were thrilled by performances from Spice Girl Mel C, Barbara Dickson, Tony Christie, former Atomic Kitten Natasha Hamilton, the Christians, comedian Jimmy Tarbuck and others.

About a week after the concert, another fund-raising event – Walk for Rhys – was organised by Liverpool fan Steven Galloway. The walk, which marked the first anniversary of Rhys's death, started at St George's Plateau, then proceeded to Stanley Park via Everton and Liverpool football grounds.

Once again there was a massive show of unity between Everton and Liverpool supporters. Children and families wearing blue and red joined

United for Rhys: Tom Woolley from Liverpool Unites (top picture, far right) gives Rhys's parents a cheque for £100,000 on derby day, while the Walk for Rhys, organised by Steven Galloway, drew supporters of both clubs (right)

95

hands as they left St George's Plateau and headed towards Anfield and Goodison Park. Former Everton star Ronnie Goodlass and former Liverpool midfielder Howard Gayle were among the walkers. Ronnie Goodlass paid tribute to the fans for coming together to support the event.

About three weeks later, on 14 September, more than 600 people wearing purple T-shirts and ribbons walked, jogged or ran a 4km course around Croxteth Park. The funds raised from sponsorship and entry fees from the Run for Rhys event were all donated to the community centre project.

THE 'LIVERPOOL UNITES' MERSEYSIDE DERBY

On 27 September 2008 Rhys Jones would have celebrated his 13th birthday. It was also the date of the Merseyside derby at Goodison Park. Appropriately, therefore, the *Liverpool Echo* chose this day to present a cheque for £100,000 to Rhys's parents, the amount that the Liverpool Unites programme had finally reached. As Alastair Machray, editor of the *Liverpool Echo* explained: 'The derby is the most important event in Liverpool's football calendar. What better opportunity to bring both sides of the city together?'

The two clubs rose to the occasion. In a show of unity, the teams warmed up wearing Liverpool Unites T-shirts while David Moyes, Rafael Benitez and the ground staff all wore purple ribbons.

Perhaps 'Liverpool Unites' could be a fitting epitaph for young Rhys Jones, whose untimely death has been, and continues to be, a powerful catalyst for goodwill and harmony between thousands of people. As Mark Thomas, editor of the *Daily Post*, so aptly puts it:

> 'The only real positive to come out of it has been the way the Merseyside community has responded to it. The way people here come together at times like this is extraordinary, and reminds us all of the sense of community that is still so strong here.'

It is difficult to think of a more suitable ending for this chapter than Mark Thomas's words about the playing of 'Z-Cars' at Anfield:

> 'It would be nice to think that it was a moment that might herald a return to the more friendly spirit of rivalry that used to prevail between fans of the two clubs. If so, it would certainly be a fitting, lasting and entirely appropriate memorial to a football-mad youngster.'

Paying respects: The Everton squad read tributes to Rhys

CHAPTER 14
TROOPING THE COLOUR:
WEARERS OF BOTH SHIRTS

Despite the Split of 1892, when Everton and Liverpool went their separate ways, there has been no reluctance by the clubs to engage in transfer deals with each other. Although there was a temporary freeze between 1962 and 1982, no fewer than 25 players have made the direct switch across Stanley Park: 17 from Everton to Liverpool, eight in the opposite direction. To this day Liverpool have signed more players from Everton than any other club.

Remarkably, 49 players have been on the books of the two clubs and 33 of these have made senior appearances for both. This chapter will give information about the 33. Rather than an alphabetical list, they have been grouped according to the era in which they played. This gives a clearer picture of the volume of traffic between the clubs at different periods.

Unfortunately space only permits more detailed accounts of a limited number of selected players in each era. However, Everton and Liverpool statistics are given for all.

THE POST-SPLIT DECADE

EDGAR CHADWICK
A superstar of his day. Born in Blackburn, 14 June 1869, Chadwick joined Everton from Blackburn Rovers in July 1888 at the start of the inaugural season of the Football League. He was the only player to feature in every Everton match that season and was also the leading scorer. He forged a formidable partnership with Alf Milward on the left wing and both were ever-presents in Everton's League championship-winning team of the 1890/91 season. They were also in Everton's losing FA Cup final sides of 1893 and 1897. In his 11 seasons with Everton, Chadwick made 300 appearances and scored 110 goals, one of only eight players ever to reach treble figures for the club. He also won seven England caps as an Everton player.

Chadwick left the Blues for Burnley in 1899, then moved on to Southampton in August 1890. He tasted his third defeat in an FA Cup final when he was on Southampton's losing side against Sheffield United in April 1902. He joined Liverpool the following month. Chadwick made 45 appearances for the Reds and scored seven goals before leaving for Blackpool in May 1904. After spells with Blackpool, Glossop and Darwen, he retired in 1908 to take up coaching in Germany. It is believed that he was the first Englishman to coach abroad. Chadwick died in Blackburn on 14 February 1942 at the age of 72.

FRED GEARY
Born in Hysen Green, Nottinghamshire, on 23 January 1868, Fred Geary was one of the trickiest and most prolific marksmen of his generation. He joined Everton from Notts Rangers in July 1889 and scored 25 goals in 20 matches in his first season for the Blues. He had phenomenal pace and a

Early movers: Edgar Chadwick (left) was one of the first players to play for both Everton and Liverpool, as was Fred Geary (above)

lethal shot, and was part of the formidable Everton front line that won the league championship in 1890/91. He went on to score 86 goals in his 98 appearances for Everton and played twice for England before moving to Liverpool in May 1895.

Geary was in the Liverpool team that won the Second Division championship in 1895/96. He scored 14 goals in 45 appearances for the Reds before injury brought his playing career to an end in 1899. Afterwards, he became the licensee of a Liverpool public house until his retirement in 1946. Geary died on 8 January 1955 in his 87th year.

PATRICK GORDON

Born in Glasgow in 1865, Gordon was a speedy right-winger who joined Everton from Renton FC, Scotland, in August 1890. A member of the Everton side that lost to Wolverhampton Wanderers in the 1893 FA Cup final, he made 23 appearances for the Blues, scoring five goals. Transferred to Liverpool in July 1893, he made 30 appearances, and scored eight goals for the Reds. Gordon left Liverpool for Blackburn Rovers in October 1894.

ANDREW HANNAH

Born in Renton, Scotland, on 17 September 1864. Hannah was the first man to captain both Everton and Liverpool. A strong full-back and a Scottish international, he joined Everton in August 1889 from Renton FC for whom he played in three Scottish Cup finals. Hannah made 47 appearances for Everton and captained the side to the 1890/91 league championship before returning to Renton the following season.

Hannah joined Liverpool in August 1892 in time for the start of their first-ever season, and captained them to the championship of the Lancashire League. The following season he was captain of Liverpool's Second Division championship-winning team. Hannah played 44 games for Liverpool and scored one goal before leaving to join Rob Roy FC in October 1895. He died on 29 May 1940 in Clydebank, Scotland.

DUNCAN McLEAN

Born in Dumbarton on 12 September 1869. McLean was a full-back who joined Everton from Renton FC in October 1890, making 26 appearances. He moved to Liverpool in 1892 and was a member of the 1893/94 Second Division championship-winning team. Overall, he made 60 appearances and scored five goals. McLean left for St Bernard's FC in October 1895.

JOHN WHITEHEAD

Born in Liverpool in 1871. Whitehead was a goalkeeper who joined Everton from Bootle FC in September 1893. He made two appearances before moving to Liverpool in March 1894, where he made his debut in April in the test match (play-off) against Bury. Liverpool lost, costing them their place in the First Division. He stayed with Liverpool until 1896 and made three appearances.

TOM WYLIE

Born in Maybole, Ayrshire, on 5 August 1870. A forward, Wylie joined Everton from Glasgow Rangers in November 1890. He made 21 appearances and scored 20 goals. Wylie moved to Liverpool in 1892 to become the club's first professional, and he scored 16 goals in 25 appearances before moving to Bury in 1893.

FROM RECONCILIATION IN 1902 TO THE FIRST WORLD WAR

ARTHUR BERRY

Born in Liverpool on 3 January 1888. The son of Edwin Berry, Liverpool chairman between 1904 and 1909, Arthur Berry's position was outside right. He joined Liverpool in April 1908 from Oxford University and made three appearances before leaving for Fulham in 1909. He then moved to Everton in the same season, where he made 29 appearances and struck seven goals. Berry left Everton for Wrexham in 1911, then played for Oxford City, and moved back to Liverpool for a second spell in October 1912. He made one appearance before returning to Wrexham in December. A brilliant amateur, Berry won one England cap and Olympic gold medals for football in 1908 and 1912.

HAROLD UREN

Born in Bristol on 23 August 1885. Uren played outside left and signed for Liverpool as an amateur from Wrexham FC in October 1907. He turned professional in 1909, made 45 appearances and scored two goals. Uren moved to Everton in February 1912 where he scored three goals in 24 appearances before leaving for Wrexham in May 1913.

TOMMY GRACIE

Born in Glasgow on 12 June 1889. The striker signed for Everton from Greenock Morton in March 1911 and scored one goal in 13 appearances. Gracie joined Liverpool in February 1912, and after 34 appearances and five goals he moved to Hearts in 1914.

ABE HARTLEY

Born in Dumbarton on 8 February 1872. Hartley was a forward who joined Everton from Dumbarton FC in December 1892. After 61 appearances and 28 goals he moved to Liverpool in December 1897, where he scored once in 12 appearances. He left Liverpool for Southampton in May 1898.

BILLY LACEY

Born in Wexford, Ireland, on 24 September 1889. Lacey's first club was Shelbourne FC in Ireland. He signed for Everton in May 1908, playing in midfield and up front. He made 40 appearances for Everton and scored 11 goals. As an Everton player he won 10 caps for Ireland. In February 1912 he moved to Liverpool where he enjoyed great success in his 259 appearances for the club. He was an FA Cup finalist in 1914 and a member of the league championship-winning teams of 1922 and 1923. In his 12 years with Liverpool he scored 29 goals and played 13 times for Ireland, thus becoming the first player to be capped with both clubs. He left Liverpool for New Brighton in June 1934 but a year later returned to Ireland, playing first for Shelbourne, then Cork Bohemians. He retired as a player in 1931 aged 42.

Lacey was described as "a rounded, lovable personality whose jutting chin was the delight of the cartoonists". He died on 30 May 1969 in his 80th year.

DAVID MURRAY

Born in Glasgow in December 1882. Murray played as a full-back, joining Everton from Glasgow Rangers in September 1903. He made two appearances, then moved to Liverpool in August 1904. Part of the team that won the Second Division championship in 1905, Murray made 15 appearances for the Reds before moving to Hull City in November 1905.

DONALD SLOAN

Born in Rankinston, Ayr, on 31 July 1883. Sloan was a goalkeeper who joined Everton from Belfast Distillery in April 1906. He made six appearances before signing for Liverpool in May 1908, where he made a further six appearances before leaving, in July 1909, to become player-manager of Distillery.

THE INTER-WAR YEARS

DICK FORSHAW

Born in Preston on 20 August 1895 but brought up in Gateshead. Forshaw was one of the most consistent forwards of his day and was the first player to win league championship medals with both Everton and Liverpool. After guest appearances with various clubs during the First World War, he joined Liverpool in July 1919. In his eight

Going for gold: Arthur Berry won two Olympic gold medals for football

seasons with the club he enjoyed great success, being ever-present in the league championship-winning sides of 1922 and 1923. He played 288 times for Liverpool and scored 124 goals. He signed for Everton in March 1927. The following season he was in the side that won the league championship, playing alongside Dixie Dean. Forshaw made 41 Everton appearances and scored eight goals before moving on to Wolverhampton Wanderers in August 1929 for one season. After short spells with Hednesford Town and Rhyl Athletic, he retired in 1931.

BILL HARTILL

Born in Wolverhampton on 18 July 1905. A centre-forward, Hartill joined Everton from Wolves in July 1935, made five appearances, scored one goal, and then moved to Liverpool in January 1936. He made five appearances at Liverpool before leaving for Bristol Rovers in March 1936.

TOMMY JOHNSON

Born in Dalton-in-Furness, Barrow, on 19 August 1901. Tommy ('Tosh') Johnson was one of the foremost players in England in his day. Prior to his move to Everton in March 1930 he had enjoyed considerable success with Manchester City, with whom he was an FA Cup runner-up in 1926 and a Second Division championship winner in 1928. His 28 league goals for City in 1928/29 and his aggregate 158 league goals are still club records. He won two England caps with City.

At Everton, Johnson formed a lethal partnership with Dixie Dean. He was a regular in the Second Division championship side of 1930/31 and in the league championship side the following season. He was also an FA Cup-winner in 1933. In 159 Everton appearances he scored 64 goals and was capped three times for England.

In March 1934 Johnson crossed Stanley Park to Liverpool. In 38 games for the Reds he scored eight goals before moving on to Darwen in August 1936. He retired a year later. Johnson died on 29 January 1973 aged 71.

NEIL McBAIN

Born in Campbeltown, Scotland, on 15 November 1895. McBain joined Everton from Manchester United on 23 January 1923 and was a midfielder. He made 103 appearances, scoring one goal. McBain left for St Johnstone in June 1926 before moving to Liverpool in March 1928, where he made 12 appearances. He moved to Watford in November 1928 and, latterly, turned out for New Brighton in goal aged 54 years and four months on 15 March 1947 – still a league age record.

FRANK MITCHELL

Born in Elgin, Scotland, on 25 May 1890. Mitchell was a goalkeeper who signed for Everton from Motherwell in May 1913. After 24 appearances he joined Liverpool on 3 February 1921. There, he made 18 appearances before leaving for Tranmere Rovers in June 1923.

FROM WORLD WAR TWO TO PREMIERSHIP LAUNCH

GARY ABLETT

Born in Liverpool on 19 November 1965. Ablett, a full-back, became a Liverpool apprentice in 1982 and turned professional in November 1983. He scored one goal in 146 appearances, winning the league championship in 1988 and 1990, and the FA Cup in 1989. Ablett signed for Everton in

January 1992. He made 156 appearances for the Blues, scoring six goals, and won the FA Cup in 1995. He moved to Birmingham City in July 1996.

PETER BEARDSLEY

Born in Newcastle-upon-Tyne on 18 January 1961. A top-quality striker gifted with close ball control and tricky dribbling skills. Beardsley was signed by Liverpool in July 1987 for nearly £2 million from Newcastle United, where he had formed a formidable strike partnership with Kevin Keegan and won 15 England caps. At Liverpool he formed another lethal partnership with Ian Rush. He played a significant part in the Liverpool team that won the league championship in 1988 and were runners-up in the FA Cup. In his 155 appearances for the Reds, Beardsley scored 59 goals and won 35 England caps.

He moved across Stanley Park to Everton at the age of 30 in August 1991 for £1 million. Although he had been very popular with the Reds' fans, he didn't find favour with new manager Graeme Souness. Looking back on the transfer, he recalled: "To be fair, the people of Merseyside were very receptive and respectful. I must have received a thousand letters from both Reds and Blues when I moved, but only one was bad. A lot of the letters I received from Liverpool supporters told me how disappointed they were that I had left but that they wished me good luck in the future."

At Everton he became only the second player after David Johnson to score the winning goal for both clubs in a Merseyside derby. It was something of which he was immensely proud: "I never dreamed that could have happened when I first signed for Liverpool, but it was an honour to play for both sides full stop. To score a winning goal in a derby for both is very special." In his 93 appearances for Everton, Beardsley scored 32 times. He left to return to Newcastle United in June 1993 for a fee of £1.45 million. He subsequently had short spells with Bolton Wanderers, Manchester City, Fulham and Hartlepool United before retiring in May 1999. He became a Newcastle coach in 2000.

STEVE McMAHON

Born in Liverpool on 20 August 1961. The midfielder became an Everton apprentice in 1977, turning professional in 1979. He made 120 appearances for the Blues and scored 14 goals before moving to Aston Villa in May 1983. He signed for Liverpool in September 1985, scoring 50 goals in 276 appearances. McMahon left for Manchester City in December 1991.

TONY McNAMARA

Born in Liverpool on 3 October 1929. McNamara played outside-right. He signed on as an Everton apprentice in July 1947, turning professional in May 1950. He made 113 appearances and scored 22 goals for the club. He

Red to Blue: Peter Beardsley crossed Stanley Park in 1991

moved to Liverpool in December 1957, where he made 10 appearances and scored three goals before signing for Crewe Alexandra in July 1958.

JOHNNY MORRISSEY

Born in Liverpool on 18 April 1940. Morrissey was a pacy, skilful winger with a deadly shot. An England schoolboy international, he signed professional forms with Liverpool in April 1957. His main position at Anfield was outside-left, but as Alan A'Court was first choice, it restricted Morrissey to only 37 appearances and six goals in his five seasons with the Reds. He switched to Everton in August 1962, a move that transformed his career. He won league championship medals in 1963 and 1970 and an FA Cup runners-up medal in 1968. He made 314 appearances for the Blues and scored 50 goals. After almost 10 years at Goodison Park he left to join Oldham Athletic in May 1972 but retired through injury a few months later.

JIMMY PAYNE

Born in Bootle on 10 March 1926. Payne signed professional forms with Liverpool in 1944 and played as a striker, scoring 43 times in 243 appearances. He moved to Everton in April 1956, but after only six appearances and two goals retired through injury in February 1957.

KEVIN SHEEDY

Born in Builth Wells on 21 October 1959. Signed for Liverpool from Hereford United in June 1978 but struggled to get into the first team. He made his debut in February 1981 but only managed four more appearances and two goals before moving to Everton in August 1982. From that point his career took off. A versatile player, he made 349 appearances for the Blues and scored 93 goals. He was a pivotal figure in Everton's many successes in the 1980s, collecting a European Cup Winners' Cup medal in 1985, league championship medals in 1985 and 1987, and FA Cup runners-up medals in 1985, 1986 and 1989. His key attributes were a long-distance lethal shot, deadly free-kicks and pin-point passing ability. Sheedy won 45 Republic of Ireland caps, 41 of them with Everton. After 10 good seasons with the club he eventually left for Newcastle United on a free transfer in February 1992. A season later he moved to Blackpool before retiring in 1995 to take up coaching.

DAVE HICKSON

A Merseyside football legend. Born in Ellesmere Port on 30 October 1929, Hickson signed as an amateur with Everton in 1947 before turning professional in May 1948. Nicknamed 'The Cannonball Kid' for his unstoppable shots, he was a dashing centre-forward with tireless energy and superb heading skills. When he left Everton for Aston Villa in September 1955 he had played 151 times for the Blues and scored 71 goals. No wonder their fans were dismayed at his departure. However, he returned to Goodison Park in July 1957, signing from Huddersfield Town.

Wing king: Kevin Sheedy only managed five appearances at Liverpool before moving to Everton, where he was a great success

In his second spell at Everton he made 92 appearances and scored 40 goals.

Hickson left Everton a second time, moving to Liverpool in November 1959 for whom he made 67 appearances and scored 38 goals. He then signed for Bury in July 1961 before a move to Tranmere Rovers in July 1962. After spells with a number of non-league clubs as player-manager then manager, Hickson left the game in 1974. Many years later he returned to Goodison Park as a stadium guide and matchday host.

DAVID JOHNSON

Born in Liverpool on 23 October 1951, the forward signed on as an Everton apprentice in April 1967, turning professional in April 1969. He made 58 appearances and scored 15 goals. Johnson moved to Ipswich in November 1972, then signed for Liverpool in August 1976 for a club

The Cannonball Kid: Dave Hickson left Everton twice, the second time for Liverpool, but returned years later to act as a stadium guide and matchday host

record fee of £200,000. In his six seasons with Liverpool he made 204 appearances and scored 78 goals, winning a European Cup winner's medal in 1981; league championship medals in 1977, 1979 and 1980; and an FA Cup runners-up medal in 1977. Returned to Everton in August 1982, making 45 appearances and scoring five goals. Johnson left for Manchester City in March 1984 after a loan spell with Barnsley.

THE PREMIERSHIP ERA

NICK BARMBY

Born in Hull, 11 February 1974. Comfortable in midfield or as a striker, Barmby started his career with Tottenham Hotspur, signing as a professional in April 1991. He was capped twice by England in his four seasons with the club. He left Spurs for Middlesbrough in August 1995 where he picked up eight more England caps before moving to Everton in November 1996 for a club record fee of £5.75 million. He played 133 games for Everton, scoring 24 goals, and winning another five England caps before moving to Liverpool for £6 million in July 2000. He made a dream start at Liverpool. In his very first season he was a member of the squad that won the FA Cup, League Cup and UEFA Cup treble. However, the bubble quickly burst as he made only 12 appearances for the Reds the following season. He stayed in favour with the England selectors, however, and added eight more caps to his tally while at Anfield. He was transferred to Leeds United in August 2002. He signed for his hometown club, Hull City, in July 2004 and played a major part in the club's promotion to the Premier League in 2007/08.

DAVID BURROWS

Born in Dudley on 25 October 1968. The defender signed for Liverpool from West Bromwich Albion in October 1988, making 193 appearances and scoring three goals. Burrows was a league championship winner in 1990 and an FA Cup winner in 1992. He left for West Ham in September 1993 but joined Everton a year later, making 23 appearances for the Blues. Moved to Coventry City in March 1995.

DON HUTCHISON

Born in Gateshead on 9 May 1971. Hutchison was a midfielder who joined Liverpool from Hartlepool United in November 1990. He made 60 appearances for the Reds and scored 10 goals before moving to West Ham in August 1994, then Sheffield United, from where he was signed by Everton in February 1998. He made 87 appearances and scored 11 goals for Everton before leaving for Sunderland in July 2000.

ABEL XAVIER

The only player to have the distinction of appearing in both Merseyside derbies in the same season. Born in Mozambique on 30 November 1972, the defender was a Portuguese international. He joined Everton from PSV Eindhoven in September 1999, made 49 appearances, and then moved to Liverpool in January 2002. In 21 appearances for the Reds he scored two goals. Xavier signed for Galatasaray in August 2003 after a loan period with the club.

SANDER WESTERVELD

Born in Enschede, Netherlands, on 23 October 1974. Westerveld was a goalkeeper who joined Liverpool from Vitesse Arnhem on 15 June 1999. He made 103 appearances before leaving for Real Sociedad on 17 December 2001. Westerveld was loaned to Everton by Portsmouth from 23 February to 8 May 2006, and he made two Premiership appearances for the Blues.

CHAPTER 15
BEN CHAMBERS: LAST OF THE SUMMER WINE

In this, the final chapter of the book, we start where we finished — in 'Summer Wine' country in the Yorkshire village of Shepley, boyhood home of Ben Chambers. Wanting to find out as much as I could about this remarkable clergyman who set the ball rolling that led to the birth of Everton and Liverpool Football Clubs, I followed his trail from cradle to grave. It was an exciting journey and took me to many interesting places but it ended with a great shock. On discovering that Chambers was laid to rest in Trinity Cemetery, Shepley, after his death in Leeds on 28 November 1901, I immediately set out to look for his grave and pay my respects. When I found it, I was horrified by the sight that met my eyes. Expecting to see a well-tended grave in a picturesque country churchyard, I found instead a sadly neglected, bramble-covered plot with almost illegible lettering on dirty, partly broken stonework. And this was just a few days after impenetrable bramble bushes and invading trees had been cut back! It was obvious that the grave of the man who had played such a vital role in the creation of two of the world's greatest football clubs had not been tended for years.

BILL KENWRIGHT AND RICK PARRY RESPOND

I informed Everton chairman Bill Kenwright and Liverpool chief executive Rick Parry of my discovery and suggested that the two clubs should combine to restore the grave and re-dedicate it at a public ceremony. I felt this would not only lend dignity to Chambers' final resting place, but would also be an opportunity for the clubs to publicly acknowledge their shared heritage and show the essential goodwill that exists between them. The suggestion met with instant approval.

Rick Parry remarked in the press:

> 'Whatever your allegiances, you can't get away from the fact that there are historic links between the Reds and the Blues on Merseyside. It's only right that his grave is properly restored as a sign of respect for the role he played in establishing football in our city.'

And Bill Kenwright stated in the *Evertonian*:

> 'Both Everton and Liverpool have a proud footballing heritage and the history of the two clubs is a source of immense pride to supporters whatever colour they choose to wear. Therefore it is entirely appropriate that we honour such a man, especially in Liverpool's Capital of Culture year.'

THE RESTORATION OF CHAMBERS' GRAVE

Once permission had been obtained to restore the grave, it was decided that it should be returned to its original state, retaining the simplicity that Chambers would have wanted. The clubs also felt that the work should be

Teaming up: Sir Philip Carter, life president of Everton FC, and Rick Parry, chief executive of Liverpool FC, shake hands at Chambers' grave

Key discovery: *Across The Park* author Peter Lupson uncovers Ben Chambers' unkempt grave in Shepley (left)
Right: Celebrating the new grave with restorer Chris Ledwidge

given to a local Yorkshire firm. Monuscript Stonemasons of Mirfield were duly entrusted with the restoration.

The site was cleared and the stonework transported to Monuscript's workshop where it was cleaned to reveal the original white marble. Unfortunately, one of the kerbstones had been damaged beyond repair by the roots of a tree and an exact replica had to be made. The inscriptions on the kerbstones with details about Chambers and his wife, Elizabeth, were then re-cut and re-painted. When the work was finished, the grave looked exactly as it had done in 1901 when Chambers' funeral took place.

The only addition was a new wedge-shaped white marble memorial tablet placed at the foot of the grave with the inscription: 'In memory of the Reverend Ben Swift Chambers who set the ball rolling that led to the birth of Everton and Liverpool Football Clubs.' The lettering was in the same style as the other inscriptions.

EVERTON AND LIVERPOOL TOGETHER AT THE COMMEMORATION SERVICE

It was very moving to discover that three Everton and three Liverpool players had carried John Houlding's coffin at his funeral in 1902 as a mark

of respect for the man who had once been the driving force behind their clubs. It was a magnificent gesture of forgiveness and reconciliation following the split 10 years earlier. It was also one that could easily be re-enacted at the service for Chambers in Shepley where the presence of three players from each club would be a public acknowledgement of a shared heritage and an expression of unity and goodwill. I put this to Bill Kenwright and Rick Parry, and was delighted that they agreed.

It was decided that player representation should span the generations, from past greats to promising stars of the future. Goalscoring legend Graeme Sharp was appointed to represent former Everton players, while Liverpool were represented by former midfield ace Brian Hall. Both had met many times before in numerous derby encounters. They were accompanied by Cory Sinnott and Michael Jensen from Everton's Academy, and Joe Kennedy and Shane O'Connor from Liverpool's.

Graeme Sharp stressed the importance of the occasion and the opportunity it presented:

> *"When you look at the history of both clubs and how they started, he was so influential. This is an ideal opportunity for us to get together and remember that. The relationship between the fans has*

deteriorated to an extent, but if we can show them there's a unity going back all those years, maybe we can restore some of that."

The service of commemoration took place at 2pm on Wednesday 2 July 2008 at Shepley Methodist Church, 2 July being the date that Ben Chambers was officially welcomed as minister of St Domingo's in Everton 131 years earlier. Club chaplains Henry Corbett of Everton and Bill Bygroves of Liverpool conducted the service with assistance from the minister of the church, Diane Hicks. Supporters of both clubs were in the congregation.

Proceedings began with a warm welcome by Geoffrey Earnshaw, a long-serving Shepley councillor and former Football League linesman. He had officiated at both Anfield and Goodison Park. During the service addresses were given by Sir Philip Carter, life president of Everton, Liverpool chief executive Rick Parry, and myself.

In his address, Sir Philip paid the following tribute to Chambers:

> "There are few things more important on Merseyside than football. Both Liverpool and Everton have a proud heritage, and the history of our clubs is a source of immense pride to our supporters. To honour a gentleman who was so pivotal to the creation of football in our city

is entirely appropriate. Ben Chambers was a visionary and everyone with an interest in football in Merseyside owes him a tremendous debt of gratitude."

Rick Parry added these comments:

> "Through cricket and football Ben Chambers showed his commitment to getting young boys off the street. He did not see football and faith as incongruous, but rather as complementary. On behalf of Liverpool and our neighbours Everton we salute this caring and committed Christian man."

When the service was over, the congregation proceeded to Trinity Cemetery led by Diane Hicks and the club chaplains, followed by the three Everton and three Liverpool players. They, in turn, were followed by Sir Philip Carter and Rick Parry.

There was a brief but moving ceremony in the cemetery, where Bill Bygroves and Henry Corbett, flanked by the players, formally re-dedicated Ben Chambers' grave.

REACTIONS TO THE DAY
The spirit of warmth and mutual respect between the clubs left a deep

Shepley Methodist Church: The joint Everton and Liverpool memorial service to Ben Chambers was held here

Below: Where Ben Chambers died – 2 Shaw St, Leeds

Right: The order of service

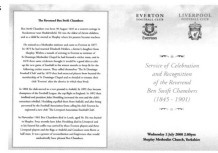

impression and many people expressed their appreciation for a memorable and inspiring day. Brian Hall commented: "It has reminded me of the wonderful rapport between Everton and Liverpool fans over so many years."

After the ceremony of re-dedication in the cemetery, one elderly Shepley resident approached me and said with tears in his eyes: "I've lived in Shepley all my life and knew nothing about this great man. I'm so proud to be from the same village as him."

It is remarkable that so little is known about a person who was instrumental in the creation of two of the country's top football clubs. No biography of Chambers has ever been written, nor has any photograph of him been discovered. But at long last, thanks to Everton and Liverpool, his name has been rescued from obscurity and he has been given a memorial worthy of his life and achievements.

Perhaps the best way of finishing this chapter, and this book, is to leave readers with a picture of the man that Chambers was. This extract from his obituary in the Methodist New Connexion conference minutes of 1902 gives us some understanding of the qualities of character that made him so special:

> 'Not only was he every inch a man, he was likewise, to the fullest measure, a Christian. His childlike faith in our Lord Jesus Christ was the blessing of his religious life.
>
> 'He was a manly, affectionate, kindly, pleasant, happy, noble being, possessing a powerful and winning personality, faithful in all the relations of life, attentive to all duties, eager to serve, anxious to do good, delighting with child-like glee in the success of his friends, hospitable, a never-failing friend, and an honourable but formidable foe. He hated sectarianism with all the energy of his strong nature, preferring the welfare of the Christian religion as a whole to any or all denominational interests. He was one of the best of husbands and a model father.
>
> 'He went to every Circuit determined to do his best. He was in energy untiring. He was a wise ruler, never allowing a meeting to get out of hand, getting through business quickly and discreetly.
>
> 'His whole soul was in his preaching. His voice was rich, sweet and powerful, his modulation excellent, his expression clear and distinct, and his energy of speech was manifest to all. He possessed a noble presence and a delivery that charmed.

'Any subject to which he gave attention was soon mastered, and he could state his views with clearness, brevity and force.

'All the great movements, such as that of education and temperance, found in him an earnest and able champion and an energetic supporter.

'For over four years he lingered in the awful grip of a fell disease; for some time he hoped against hope, being eager to recover, that he might again engage in his beloved work of preaching, but when the position was once realised he surrendered himself to the will of God with uncomplaining resignation, longing to depart and be with Christ, which is far better. The patience with which he bore his affliction was exemplary.

'[He] died at Leeds on the 28th November 1901, being interred at Shepley three days later, amid genuine manifestations of sorrow by a large concourse of people gathered from near and distant places to pay a last homage to one who had gained their respect and attachment.'

Showing support: Graeme Sharp and Brian Hall at Chambers' grave (top); joined by Michael Jensen, Cory Sinnott, Shane O'Connor and Joe Kennedy from Liverpool and Everton's academies (above). Left: (l-r) Liverpool FC chaplain Bill Bygroves; Kevin Moore, the director of the National Football Museum; Peter Lupson; and Henry Corbett, chaplain of Everton FC, at Ben Chambers' grave

Other publications produced by Sport Media:

  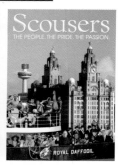

**All of these titles, and more, are available to order by calling 0845 143 0001,
or you can buy online at www.merseyshop.com**